NEW YORK
Ghost Towns

NEW YORK
Ghost Towns

UNCOVERING
THE HIDDEN PAST

SUSAN HUTCHISON TASSIN

STACKPOLE
BOOKS

Published by
STACKPOLE BOOKS
5067 Ritter Road
Mechanicsburg, PA 17055
www.stackpolebooks.com

Printed in the United States of America

10 9 8 7 6 5 4 3 2 1

FIRST EDITION

Cover photo by Chip Cain, www.creativeashes.com
Cover design by Wendy Reynolds

Library of Congress Cataloging-in-Publication Data

Tassin, Susan.
  New York ghost towns : uncovering the hidden past / Susan Hutchison Tassin. — First edition.
pages cm
  Includes bibliographical references and index.
  ISBN 978-0-8117-0825-8 (paperback)
  1. Ghost towns—New York (State)—History. 2. Historic sites—New York (State) 3. New York (State)—History, Local. I. Title.
  F120.T27 2013
  974.7—dc23
                                        2012047824

For my children, Jennifer and Joey,
for making life so much fun

CONTENTS

Northeastern New York

Western New York

PREFACE

I will reluctantly admit to formerly being a bit ignorant when it came to New York State. Even though I grew up just an hour south from its border in north-central Pennsylvania, most of my traveling had been south. My knowledge of New York, I'm chagrined to say, consisted of school field trips to the Corning Museum of Glass, vacations to Niagara Falls, shopping jaunts to New York City, and as an adult, visiting the awesome wineries. Then I wrote this book.

I now rank New York State among my very favorite places on earth. I was speechless at some of the beautiful wild terrain I observed, such as the Seneca Highlands, Letchworth State Park, the Hudson River Valley, and the gorgeous Adirondack mountains. One of the most humbling realizations on my journeys through this beautiful state was how critical New York was to the infancy of this nation. Between the French and Indian War and the Revolutionary War, New York truly was the key to controlling the continent.

Aside from the inspiring natural beauty and fascinating history, I met more lovely, gracious people on my journeys than I can ever hope to thank for their assistance in this project. There are too many to name all of them, and for those omitted or who requested to be anonymous, it is not from a lack of appreciation. From docents and historical interpreters to innkeepers and winery owners, all made my trips not only extremely informative, but also enjoyable. Thank you all.

I do wish to thank my parents, Bill and Mary Hutchison, for their support. I also thank my wonderful editor, Kyle Weaver, who took a chance on an unpublished writer several years ago. I can't thank him enough for giving me the opportunity, and for agreeing with me that ghost towns were fascinating and that others would think so, too.

Thank you, Joey and Jennifer, my two children. Old enough now to accompany me, they marched through hot, muggy, occasionally spooky ghost towns without complaint and proved to be enjoyable, enthusiastic travel partners.

I also wish to thank my dear friends, Sherri Umbaugh and Heather Whitfield Swope, who assisted with some of the actual ghost-towning for this book. Sherri accompanied me on two epic trips through the state and made the journeys memorable and so much fun. Her irrational phobia of bears made for some hilarious moments. Heather was new to ghost-towning and took to it like a pro. Thanks to her, I was dissuaded from giving up on finding Tahawus, one mile short of the town. It was worth that last mile of searching, and I am grateful. She was a cheerful, enthusiastic companion on my journeys.

To the ladies at the Pioneer Oil Museum who took great pains to open the museum, drive me out to the Richburg Oil Well monument, and never complain about giving up part of their weekend to help, I am grateful. Likewise, Timmy Gardocki, the charming young man at the Beekman 1802 Mercantile in Sharon Springs, thank you for your help. I'm still disappointed that I was unable to buy any of your delicious sold-out cheese.

I also want to thank Chip Cain, president of the Harrisburg (Pa.) Camera Club for providing his considerable talent in creating the cover photo for this book, of Bannerman Island. I consider myself fortunate to have his help.

New York City Area

DOODLETOWN

In arguably one of the most beautiful locations in New York State, Doodletown is well worth the walk in from the road.

History

There are varying reports about how Doodletown received its unusual name. Some believe that the name came when British troops marched through the town on their way to fight at Forts Montgomery and Clinton, near present-day West Point. To antagonize the locals, the British soldiers sang "Yankee Doodle" as they marched past. Others believe that the name came from the Dutch term for "Dead Dell."

One of the earliest families to inhabit the area of the Hudson River Valley that would later become Doodletown was the June family. In the current ruins, there are two June family cemeteries. The first June family members, Ithiel and Charity June, arrived in the area in the early 1760s. They purchased several hundred acres from a family named Tompkins and settled in. Their neighbors included the Herbert and Weiant families. By the 1850s, the tiny settlement had been joined by several other families, including the Rhodes, Sheldons, and Kesslers.

In approximately 1854, the Mountville Presbyterian Church and an adjoining parsonage were built to serve the families of Doodletown and the surrounding areas. The church building was also used as a schoolhouse for the local children.

By the early 1870s, there were three distinct cemeteries, and more than twenty-five families lived in the hamlet. The community had grown to the point of needing a larger church, which was built in the center of town. This church was a Methodist Episcopal denomination, which was presided over by circuit ministers who traveled throughout the region. The earlier church was decommissioned and became a private home. A large one-room school was built to educate the children of the village.

Just north of Doodletown was Iona Island, an island in the Hudson River named for the Iona grapes that were grown there. By 1859, it was privately owned, including by Dr. E.W. Grant, who grew not only grapes, but also an apple orchard on the site. He owned a grand home. Later, in the 1890s, an amusement park called the Iona Island Picnic Grove was built on the island. The doctor's mansion served as a hotel for visitors. The new park and hotel provided some employment for Doodletown residents.

Around 1900, the area was being mulled over as a possible state prison site. Alarmed citizens mobilized to preserve the area. The concept of using the area instead for recreation was floated and met with enthusiasm. By 1910, the new Park Commission, housed at Bear Mountain, had begun to accumulate local land with the purpose of preserving and maintaining its beauty for future generations.

Large parcels of land were given or sold to the Park Commission by some of the wealthier landholders in the area. However, other acreage was owned by more humble landowners who did not wish to sell their property. The wheels of progress churned on, however, and little by little the land was taken, either through voluntary sales or by power of eminent domain.

Doodletown continued to thrive during the early phases of the park's development. Small villages and hamlets in the surrounding area began to be swallowed up by the park, but Doodletown was relatively untouched at first. However, by 1937, the townspeople were starting to suspect that they were in danger of being swallowed by the park as well. However, the end of Doodletown was still a few decades away.

Life in Doodletown was quiet and peaceful. Some townspeople were able to make a living within the town's boundaries, while many others commuted to work by horse, ferry, and train, and later, by automobile. As commuting became easier, it became desirable to live in Doodletown, enjoying the quiet pace of life there, while working elsewhere.

The decade leading up to 1920 was an exciting one for the area. A large dock for steamboats was constructed on the Hudson River, and the Bear Mountain Inn was built. People from other parts of the state and country began to discover the area's beauty, bringing cars in on the newly built roads and bridges. Seven Lakes Drive, one of the most scenic roads in the country, was constructed.

As the town grew, the need for a larger school became evident. The children were still using a one-room schoolhouse. In 1926, to service the higher population, a lovely two-room schoolhouse was erected. It was constructed using local fieldstone, much of which was collected by the local children. The school housed grades one through eight. Beyond eighth grade, the children had to commute to schools in other towns.

Charles Watson, a local man, devised these lyrics (set to the tune of "My Darlin' Clementine") to be sung during a PTA get-together:

> In a valley, in the mountains,
> By the Hudson, all serene,
> Lies a village, rests a hamlet,
> Snug amongst the forest's green.

Where the Indian had his way
Came a hunter one fine day,
Walked the trail and climbed the rocks,
Seeking bear and wily fox.

Then the settlers did declare,
Freedom's ring was in the air.
Came the British troops galore,
Marching Redcoats, bent on war.

Independence is what we got,
After flame and many a shot.
Then in peace we settled down,
Staked a claim in Doodletown.

Up the river to the land,
Came our small but hardy band.
Men and women, children too,
Braved the storms the north wind blew.

Felled the trees and mined the ore,
Tilled the fields and did the chores.
Stayed to see our dream come true,
House and home, and life made new.

If some laughter is what you're after,
Sing from cellar to the rafter,
Oh, my darling, don't you frown,
Sing in praise of Doodletown.

If your sorrow you'd like to drown,
Come on up to Doodletown.
Gather round and sing for fun,
Get together and sing as one.

If you've had enough of strife,
And you want a real good life,
Set your hat on straight and then,
Head right for this little glen.

Walk and ramble, run and gambol,
Travel up and travel down,
You will never, hardly ever,
Find a place like Doodletown.

If some joy you could employ,
Peace of mind you'd like to find,
Do not dilly, do not dally,
Hasten to this lovely valley.

Several small businesses were located in and near Doodletown. For example, in the 1920s there was a general store, which also served as the town's informal post office prior to the official post office opening. The Herbert family owned the store, with Mrs. Minnie Herbert serving as clerk while her husband, Oscar, was a local blacksmith. He regularly traveled to the post office in Iona Island to retrieve the town's mail and bring it to his store. In 1937 a formal post office was opened on Bear Mountain.

For recreation, the townspeople enjoyed frequent church activities and dinners. On Pleasant Valley Road, a resident named Luther Stalter often hosted square dances in his barn. Some of the locals played baseball with the local team, the Bear Mountain Bears. The baseball games were typically played in the large field adjacent to the Bear Mountain Inn. A roller- and ice-skating rink located near the Bear Mountain Inn was a popular destination for local teenagers. It stood beside Hessian Lake until it burned in 1952.

The children of the area also enjoyed a swimming hole called "The Ten Foot." It was located in Doodletown Creek and was surrounded by enormous boulders. The water was said to be extremely cold, but that didn't dampen the children's enthusiasm.

In 1918, the June-Lemmon tract of land was sold to the Park Commission. One of the park's superintendents lived in the home on this property. He was an avid gardener and planted an impressive nursery on the site. Some of the nursery plants are still present today in the surrounding woods.

Slowly, the town began to disappear, as one by one, residents sold their properties to the Park Commission. As the homeowners moved away, the Commission commandeered the land, either tearing down the buildings or renting the homes to park employees.

According to Elizabeth "Perk" Stalter, former resident and historian of the town, the Gray family lands were sold in the mid 1920s, and the Scandell tract in 1928. Some Herbert land was acquired in 1932, followed shortly thereafter by the Newell property. The venerable June family began to sell their own land by 1940.

With the outbreak of World War II, Doodletown was affected like many communities in the United States. Several of the young men in town went off to fight in the war. At least one returned with serious injuries. The remaining townspeople spent the wartime growing victory gardens and being as self-sufficient as possible. They welcomed their soldiers back with open arms at the conclusion of the war, and life returned to normal.

The end of the war, however, had one ominous implication for Doodletown. The Park Commission, which had been dormant and focused elsewhere during the war years, returned its attention to the acquisition of land in the area.

The Town Today

Thanks in large part to the efforts of Elizabeth Stalter (who wrote the definitive history of the hamlet), the disappearing Doodletown is easy to visit in a meaningful way. Although the site is difficult to locate initially, once you are on the trail to the town, it is well marked with large, detailed maps. In addition, placards are placed in front of the sites of various ruins left from the town. The town roads, while obviously unmaintained, make for an easy hike. Foundations are evident throughout the area. Three cemeteries, also easily located from the maps, are well maintained and completely intact. Plan to spend a minimum of several hours wandering around the town. Be watchful for snakes.

Directions

While driving on Seven Lakes Drive in the Palisades Interstate Park in New York, find the significant landmark of the Bear Mountain Inn. After passing the Inn, continue south on Seven Lakes Drive past the first roundabout. When the road takes a very sharp V curve, you will see a small sign for Lemmon Road on the left. This marks the beginning of the trail to the town. Parking is difficult, but there is room for one or two cars at the mouth of the trail.

Proceed down the trail. In approximately a quarter mile, you will begin seeing schematic maps clearly marking the way and delineating the locations of various buildings and cemeteries.

It is also possible to hike to the site from the second parking lot of the Bear Mountain Inn (which has a charge for parking). Follow the "white" trail through the tunnel in the back of the lot. Doodletown is reportedly a half mile hike from the lot.

ROSETON

A successful business takes up residence on the beautiful banks of the Hudson River.

History

In the mid- to late 1800s, entrepreneurs realized that the Hudson River Valley had a natural resource that would later become instrumental to the region's economy: rich clay that could be made into bricks.

In 1883, John C. Rose, who owned a small brickyard in nearby Haverstraw, decided to expand his business by purchasing a three hundred-acre parcel of land north of Newburgh. Included with his $25,000 purchase was a mansion and the surrounding land, formerly the property of the Davis family. He promptly tore down the mansion and located the new brickyard on the site. The large banks of high-quality clay quickly paid off. Rose and Company soon became a leading provider of bricks for New York City and beyond.

A town began forming around the brickyard as more and more employees were needed. At its busiest, the brickyard employed almost a thousand workers. Although some of the employees commuted from nearby towns, others moved to the area. Rose created a company town to house them. Besides homes, the hamlet contained a two-story school, a post office, a general store, churches, and even an entertainment hall, with billiards, a stage, and meeting rooms.

Rose and Company incorporated in 1884. The company ran sixteen brick machines, which could manufacture twenty-four thousand bricks per day. Each year, the brickyard produced approximately four million bricks.

Adjacent to the Rose brickyard was the Jova brickyard. Already a successful businessman, Juan Jacinto Jova reluctantly turned his family's vacation property into a profitable brick-manufacturing operation after watching the Rose family's success. Jova and his wife were instrumental in building Our Lady of Mercy Chapel in Roseton.

Under John C.'s leadership, Rose and Company (the name was later changed to The Rose Brick Company) thrived. Like his sons after him, John C. was an innovator. Prior to his involvement, barges carried bricks downriver belowdecks. A maximum load was 75,000 bricks. John C. Rose devised a way for ships to carry the bricks above decks, expanding the carrying capacity of the barges to 600,000 per load.

John C. Rose and his son Hilend managed Rose and Company for several years. However, in 1894 Hilend suddenly died. His father passed away two years later. Another of John C.'s sons, John Bailey Rose, was attending college at Yale when his father passed away. In April 1897, two months before graduation, John B. took over the business (conflicting accounts exist as to whether he officially graduated). He was twenty-two.

The company continued to prosper after John B. took over. Rose bricks were used in building the Waldorf Astoria Hotel, the New York Stock Exchange, the Empire State Building, and the Customs House of the Battery. Gravel made from ground-up Rose bricks was used to pave the lanes in Central Park.

On a typical work day, approximately one hundred and fifty horses and their handlers were needed to transport the clay to the brick machines. An innovator like his father, John B. Rose built a three mile-long private railroad that could accommodate a train with fifty railroad cars. The train could carry 750 tons of material per load. The horses and almost a hundred workers lost their jobs due to redundancy.

Brickwork was seasonal, and the winter months could be very hard on workers' families. During lean times the local store extended credit to the workers to help them survive until brickmaking season resumed. Some idle workers traveled to Rockland Lake (see page xx) to work in the ice industry during the winter.

John Bailey Rose opened a company headquarters in New York City, on West 52nd Street. He eventually entered politics, serving on the Electoral College in 1904 for Theodore Roosevelt and serving as a New York State Senator for two terms, starting in 1908.

Rose eventually closed the business and sold the land. His own home, nicknamed "The Homestead," was sold to a man named Angelo Sasso, who turned it into a restaurant named Beau Rivage. The restaurant was popular and remained open for many years until it burned down on New Year's Eve 1982. The brickyard itself was sold to the Central Hudson Gas and Electric Company. The company also bought most of the private homes in the area and promptly demolished them.

The Town Today

Little is left of what was once Roseton. The post office closed in 1970. The school building survived for some time and was used for storage by the local school district. However, it was eventually sold and demolished. The only significant building still standing is the Our Lady of Mercy Chapel, built in 1891 with sponsorship from the Jova family. It is still a well-attended church for the local Roman Catholic population, many of whom are descendants of the brick workers.

Directions

From Interstate 84 East, take Exit 10 toward Newburgh. Turn left onto US 9 West. There is a highway marker on Route 9W north of Newburgh. From there, turn right, toward the river. Our Lady of Mercy Chapel is just north of the site of Roseton.

BEDLOE'S ISLAND

Bedloe's Island went through a number of tenants and owners before becoming home to one of the country's most treasured monuments: the Statue of Liberty.

History

Native Americans were the first to spend time on what later became known as Ellis Island. The Algonquins valued the rich oyster beds located on the island; in fact, Ellis Island and two neighboring islands were known as the "Oyster Islands." Archaeological evidence shows that the Indians living on the island ate the oysters and discarded the shells, which were found along with arrowheads and pottery shards. In addition, the Indians apparently varied their diet with ducks, turtles, deer, and fish, as bones of those animals were found among the oyster shells.

The Algonquin were a fairly peaceful people, and they existed alongside several other neighboring tribes throughout what are now the boroughs of New York City. It was not until the Dutch arrived in 1609 that life changed dramatically for the residents of the Oyster

Islands. Henry Hudson set up a Dutch colony along what became the Hudson River, and Native Americans began trading and working with the Europeans. The Dutch called the area New Netherlands.

The Native Americans and the Dutch struck an unusual arrangement. For three years, the Europeans were allowed to collect as many furs as they could from the area inhabited by the tribes. The Dutch then provided the Indians with tools such as iron axes, knives, farming tools, and iron pots. While this arrangement initially worked, the Native American people were not prepared for the diseases that the Europeans carried. Pestilence, war, and increasing numbers of Europeans eventually reduced the Native American presence in the area. By the mid-1600s the area was firmly controlled by the Europeans.

The English took over the area in 1664 and promptly renamed it New York. The colonial governor deeded Oyster Island to Captain Robert Needham. Three years later, on December 23, 1667, Captain Needham sold the island to a Dutch merchant and shop owner, Isaac Bedloe.

In 1669, Isaac Bedloe was informed by the new colonial governor, Francis Lovelace, that he could maintain ownership of Oyster Island under two conditions: that he allow people who were charged with civil crimes to live there, and that he rename the island after Lovelace. Bedloe agreed and named the island Love Island.

In 1673, the Dutch colonists rebelled against Lovelace. Although Bedloe had passed away, the Dutch briefly maintained control of New York, overthrowing Governor Lovelace, before the British regained control of the area. The island was renamed Bedloe's Island.

Isaac Bedloe's widow, Mary Bedloe Smith, did not fare well after her husband's death. Facing financial ruin, she sold Bedloe's Island in 1732 to local merchants Adolph Philpse and Henry Lane. Lane and Philipse quickly lost control of the island, although they retained ownership. New York used the island to inspect incoming seamen and colonists for smallpox before allowing them into the city.

In January 1746, the island was sold to Archibald Kennedy, who was the collector and receiver general for the Port of New York.

Kennedy planned to use the island as a summer retreat, a plan that briefly worked. He built a lighthouse and a home on the island in 1753, but in 1755 the city again seized control of the island for use as a quarantine center. Disgusted that his intended use of the island was thwarted, Kennedy sold the island to the city of New York in February 1758. The government quickly built a hospital (called a "pesthouse") for those suffering from smallpox.

During the American Revolution, the British maintained control of New York for some time. Bedloe's Island became a sanctuary for American colonists who remained loyal to England. However, in April 1776, American colonial forces attacked Bedloe's Island and razed the buildings on it.

In 1793, the French were given Bedloe's Island. They again used it as a quarantine and isolation station. However, the young American government began to realize that this island was in a prime position to help protect the entrance to New York Harbor. The Americans asked the French to return the island, which they did in 1796.

Fort Wood was constructed on the island in 1807. It was named for Eleazer D. Wood, an army hero who was killed in battle during the War of 1812. Fort Wood was shaped like an eleven-pointed star. It was staffed by approximately six hundred soldiers in 1851. This number of inhabitants stretched the resources of the fort to the limit, and most lived in crowded tents instead of barracks. By 1852, most soldiers were moved elsewhere. The fort was used again during the Civil War, when it served as a storage facility for weaponry. Soldiers would remain stationed on Bedloe's Island until 1937.

In 1881, construction of the Statue of Liberty began in France. The statue was designed by French sculptor August Bartholdi and was intended to represent freedom as well as to cement the friendship between the United States and France. The plan was to place the statue on Bedloe's Island, since it would be visible to all entering New York Harbor. Bartholdi liked the idea of the statue standing at the "gateway to America." The statue was completed in France by

1884. It was transported to the United States in June 1865 and was reassembled on Bedloe's Island in 1886.

Fort Wood played a role in the statue's construction: The pedestal of the statue is situated within its star-point walls.

The Town Today

The Statue of Liberty is a treasured landmark in the United States, inviting thousands to visit. At the time of publication, an interior renovation is underway, and visitors are not allowed to climb the stairs inside the statue. It is best to check ahead if planning to visit. For those interested in the history of the Bedloe's Island settlement, little remains: the fort walls are the only reminders of the island's past life.

Directions

Bedloe's Island and the Statue of Liberty are only accessible by the ferry, which departs from either Battery Park, New York, or Liberty State Park, New Jersey. Private boats are not permitted to dock on the island.

CAMP SHANKS/SHANKS VILLAGE

Camp Shanks, "Last Stop USA," was indeed the last view of the United States for thousands of servicemen who passed through this site on their way to fight in the European Theater during World War II.

History

Orangeburg, a peaceful town on the Hudson River, was a comfortable commute away from New York City in the early twentieth century. Those who didn't travel into the city every day worked as farmers and shopkeepers, making this lovely bedroom community a desirable place to live. However, in 1942 the town underwent a rapid, dramatic change. The United States was embroiled in a vicious world war, and the citizens of Orangeburg were called upon to make an astounding sacrifice to their country's war effort.

Under the War Powers Act, which gave the federal government unprecedented power, the United States government set its sights on obtaining a little over two thousand acres of land, mostly consisting of farmland, in and around Orangeburg as the site of a camp for housing troops on their way to fight overseas. The location was almost perfect: It was near train lines and shipping sites, making troop movement very easy.

On September 25, 1942, at a meeting held at the Orangeburg school, property owners were informed that their land was to be purchased for the war effort. The surprised landowners were given two weeks to leave their property, some of which had been in families for generations.

Almost overnight, Camp Shanks, named for Major General Carey Shanks, was begun. Seventeen thousand workers descended upon the area. They hastily demolished existing homes and barns and constructed more than two thousand buildings on the site. The camp, which was run by a staff of six thousand, opened for business on January 4, 1943. It was to serve as temporary housing for up to 47,000 troops at a time as they were processed to be sent overseas to fight.

While the soldiers were housed at the camp, the necessary personnel and financial paperwork was completed, health assessments were done, and uniforms were issued. The soldiers drilled and practiced and were prepared for what to expect on board the ships that would transport them. Each soldier was given a gas mask, which they were required to test in a gas chamber on the base.

By the time the base was fully functional, $43 million had been spent on construction and infrastructure. Besides the two thousand buildings, the camp also had several roads that required maintenance, a sewer system, water towers, and electrical services.

The temporary residents of Camp Shanks were carefully separated by race and gender. African-American troops had their own barracks separate from the white soldiers. They also attended a different USO club than white soldiers. The Women's Army Corps (WAC) soldiers were likewise kept in separate housing.

There were several recreational outlets for the soldiers, both in the camp and in several nearby towns. Nearby USO clubs were popular; the four that were most popular with the troops were located in Nyack, Tappan, Orangeburg, and Pearl River. Within the camp there were baseball fields, a swimming pool, a gymnasium, and a bowling alley. In addition, there were beer halls and concert venues to entertain the troops. Many popular entertainers visited Camp Shanks; Pearl Bailey, Frank Sinatra, Helen Hayes, Jackie Gleason, Shirley Temple, Judy Garland, Humphrey Bogart, Dinah Shore, and many others provided a pleasant distraction to the soldiers preparing to leave for the European Theater.

As the war continued, Camp Shanks took on a new role: that of prisoner of war camp. Italian and German soldiers were sent to Camp Shanks to remain until they could be returned to Europe. In total, 290,000 foreign prisoners of war passed through Camp Shanks. The typical POW remained at the camp for anywhere from a few weeks to several months.

Eventually, the war came to an end, and the camp became obsolete. By the summer of 1946, a new purpose was found for the camp. With the end of the war and the advent of the GI Bill, enrollment in colleges had increased dramatically. Columbia University, located in New York City, had a housing crisis as new students flooded in. A deal was struck with the US government to use some of Camp Shanks as living quarters for the students. By the time this transformation was complete, the camp had served as a departure point for 1.3 million troops, including E Company, 2nd Battalion of the 506th Infantry Regiment of the 101st Airborne, immortalized in the series *Band of Brothers.*

Approximately fifteen hundred of the Camp Shanks barracks were transformed into apartments for four thousand families. Many of the remaining empty barracks were converted into apartments for returning soldiers who did not intend to attend college. Most of the new apartments were two-bedroom units, with a living room, a kitchen, and a bathroom. To meet the needs of this new community, tennis courts, playgrounds, a library, and a community center were constructed.

Unlike Camp Shanks, Shanks Village (as the community was named) was integrated, with black and white families living in the same buildings. The village thrived and provided its residents with a safe, pleasant place to live.

By 1951, many of the collegiate GIs had graduated and moved on. Columbia University ended its sponsorship of the village and residency dwindled. The final tenants left in 1956. With the completion of both the Tappan-Zee Bridge and the Palisades Interstate Parkway, developers swooped in to build suburban housing for New York City commuters. Soon, little remained of Camp Shanks.

The Town Today

Little remains of Camp Shanks and Shanks Village today. Two monuments to their existence remain. There is a statue, the Camp Shanks Monument, in Tappan, and the Camp Shanks Museum. The museum contains many photographs of the town, as well as a diorama.

Directions

The Camp Shanks Monument is located at Independence Avenue and Lowe Lane, off Western Highway, in the city of Tappan. The Camp Shanks Museum is located on South Greenbush Road in Orangeburg. It is close to the intersection of Routes 303 and 340. It was opened in June 1994 on the fiftieth anniversary of D-day and contains artifacts, photos, and uniforms. It is open weekends from Memorial Day through Labor Day, and admission is free.

LETCHWORTH VILLAGE

Although arguably not a true town, it was nevertheless home to many people over the years.

History

Letchworth Village, which began its existence as the Eastern New York State Custodial Asylum, was eventually named Letchworth Village Home for the Feeble Minded and Epileptics, after the famous New York philanthropist, William Pryor Letchworth.

Unlike most institutions in place at the time for the mentally disabled, Letchworth Village was intended to resemble a village, as opposed to a sterile, cold institution. It had mostly one-story buildings, spaced out around the property, instead of large hospital wards. There were cottages in which the residents lived, along with dining halls, staff housing, and a hospital. The concept was that the atmosphere would be more home-like, and that feeling more comfortable and being part of a community would produce better outcomes for the patients.

The patients were separated by gender. From there, they were further separated into three groups: young and improvable, middle-aged and industrious, and infirm and helpless. The groups did not mingle.

One of the concerns with Letchworth Village was that the definition of appropriate resident was very wide. People with Down Syndrome, epileptics, microcephalics, dwarves, and even albinos were accepted. Some therapists employed by the institution were concerned that some of the children they worked with were very intelligent, and perhaps should have been educated elsewhere. Letchworth Village strove to educate and train its residents. In addition, the residents who were able were given jobs to do around the farm.

Letchworth Village struggled with issues such as underfunding from the government as well as overcrowding. Its programs were rare among such institutions and were very popular. In the late 1970s, institutions such as Letchworth Village became less popular. Initiatives to educate special-needs children in public schools began, and families opted to keep their family members within their homes. Some residents were placed in group homes.

Well-publicized reports that were harshly critical of Letchworth Village's treatment of its clientele came to light. Accusations of maltreatment of the residents were rampant, hastening the village's demise. Letchworth Village closed its doors in 1996. The farmland was sold off.

The Town Today

There are still Letchworth Village buildings standing vacant. Several buildings are in use, but none are available to tour by the public. Sources report that walking about the grounds during the day is legal, but entering the buildings is not. In addition, it is not safe to enter the buildings. Structural infirmities, hazards, and vagrants may be present.

Directions

From the Palisades Parkway, take Exit 14 toward Thiells/Haverstraw. Turn right at the bottom of the ramp onto County Route 98/Willow Grove Road. Turn right onto County Route 94/Letchworth Village Road. Turn right onto Ridge Road, and then take a right onto Underpass Road. Turn right onto Storrs Road, and then make a right onto E. Vanderlip.

FORT SCHUYLER

Now housed within the Merchant Marine Academy, Fort Schuyler once stood sentinel over New York Harbor.

History

Following the War of 1812, the United States came to the uncomfortable realization that it needed to better protect its coastlines from foreign invasion. A number of defenses were built along the East Coast. One such installation was Fort Schuyler.

Fort Schuyler was built to protect New York City from foreign intruders. It guarded the eastern entrance of New York Harbor from Long Island Sound, on Throg's Neck. The fort was situated where the East River met the sound, across from Fort Totten.

The decision to build the fort was made in 1818. The federal government purchased fifty-two acres in modern-day Bronx from William Bayard in 1826, and construction began in 1833. The fort was built using granite brought from nearby Greenwich, Connecticut. It was designed with an irregular pentagon shape and was intended to house 1,250 soldiers. From land, access was through a drawbridge, with passage through a tunnel equipped with gunslits for cutting down invaders.

By December 1845, the fort was already heavily armed, even though construction was still ongoing. In 1856, the completed fort was inducted into service. It was named Fort Schuyler after General Philip Schuyler, who had led the Continental forces in the early stages of the Saratoga Campaign in 1777. During the Civil War, the fort was used to house approximately five hundred prisoners of war, including some Union soldiers who had been arrested for various crimes.

The fort included the MacDougall Hospital, which contained two thousand beds. The hospital, and indeed the entire fort, was exceptional in its cleanliness and ability to adequately dispose of waste. In the time that the fort was in use, not a single man was lost to disease. In May 1934, the last soldiers left the fort. Work began to incorporate the fort as part of the New York State Merchant Marine Academy.

The Town Today

The fort is open for unguided walking tours (information and maps are provided at the visitor center). The fort functions as a museum not only for Fort Schuyler's history, but also an underwater artifacts exhibit, a modern shipping exhibit, and the maritime academy. Not open to the public are the tunnels and dungeons that are rumored to lie beneath the fort.

The fort and museum are open daily Monday through Saturday, from 9 A.M. to 4 P.M. Admission and parking are free.

Directions

From Brooklyn, Queens, and Long Island by way of Throg's Neck Bridge: Use the extreme right toll booth and exit immediately on your right after paying toll. Continue to the second stop sign and turn left, crossing over the expressway and bearing left onto Pennyfield Avenue. Take Pennyfield Avenue to the end. The college's front gate is to the left.

CAMP HERO

Was Long Island home to experiments in time travel, mind control, and teleportation?

History

The origins of Camp Hero were relatively "normal." The far eastern end of Long Island had long been viewed as a potentially strategic site for the military. However, the United States government was pressed to take action on the site following the Japanese attack on Pearl Harbor in 1941. The base was initially named Camp Hero and was intended to monitor the area for Nazi submarines, which were considered to be a significant threat to the East Coast. The facility included bunkers.

Initially, the base was disguised as a small civilian fishing port, and few outsiders recognized it for what it was. When the war ended in 1945, the base's staffing was reduced, and the government talked of closing it. However, in the face of a perceived increase in threat level from the Soviets, the government ramped up staffing at the base. By 1948, surveillance, including a new radar installation, was in full swing, searching for possible Soviet infiltration. Camp Hero was first renamed Montauk Point, then was changed again in 1953 to Montauk Air Force Station.

The Montauk Air Force Station kept watch for Soviet invasions through 1978. However, as satellite technology improved and replaced radar surveillance, the base became obsolete. President Jimmy Carter ordered the base to be closed. It was soon afterward that a rogue group of scientists started using the facility for forbidden experiments—or so the stories say.

To understand how the strange rumors about Camp Hero began, one must first understand the Philadelphia Experiment, a supposed experiment in teleportation. The Philadelphia Experiment, also known as the Rainbow Project, was conducted in the Philadelphia Naval Yard in October 1943. The U.S. Navy was reportedly working on developing invisibility using a modified version of Albert Einstein's Unified Field Theory. The prevailing belief was that if we could make our warships invisible to radar, our enemies would quickly surrender. However, the unexpected result of the experiment, stories say, was actual teleportation.

The experiment involved a Navy warship, the DE 173 USS *Eldridge*. As the experiment progressed, the ship became invisible to the crew, who could no longer see the deck below their feet. The ship supposedly teleported to Norfolk, Virginia, and then back to Philadelphia several minutes later.

Eyewitnesses allegedly observed the *Eldridge*'s disappearance and reappearance. From a nearby steamer, Navy personnel saw the air around the warship darken, followed by the appearance of a strange green mist. At that point, the ship abruptly disappeared, reappearing several minutes later.

However, the experiment did not go smoothly. When the ship rematerialized in Philadelphia, several crew members never reappeared. Others made the journey, but were welded fatally into the metal of the ship. Those who returned physically unscathed were mentally disoriented and unstable. They were discharged with a mental health diagnosis. Few remembered or talked about their ordeal, and those that did were considered to be psychotic and were largely ignored.

According to some, the U.S. government quickly ended its research into radar invisibility and teleportation at this point. The difficulties in keeping witnesses quiet, the challenges in explaining the disappearances of sailors, and the realization that the technology was far too mysterious and undeveloped to pursue influenced the decision.

Less than a decade later, the Philadelphia Experiment scientists met secretly to discuss options. They believed that the importance of the invisibility and teleportation experiments could not be ignored. In addition, they believed that it was crucial to explore the devastating psychological damage to the members of the *Eldridge*'s crew. They thought that harnessing the power that damaged the crew could be used on enemy forces in the form of mind control.

Congress refused to fund the program, concerned about the consequences of engaging in this mysterious research. The story holds that powerful military leaders at the Pentagon ignored Congress's refusal and began a project in secret, unable to ignore the potential military advantages of the technology. Because of the secrecy that was necessary, the funding for the project had to be similarly secret. The stories say that the funding was obtained from Nazi gold that had been recovered from a train stopped in France near the end of World War II.

The scientists initially set up shop at the Brookhaven National Laboratory on Long Island. Then the team, anxious to pursue their mind control experiments, decided that they needed a large radar dish. They quickly realized that an unused radar dish was located at nearby Camp Hero in Montauk. They quietly set up shop, building an extensive system of underground laboratories so that the research could be conducted in complete secrecy.

The theories about the experiments tend to center on the use of various frequencies, and the study of how they altered moods. The goal was to train brain waves and use them strategically. One of the mind control experiments conducted at Camp Hero supposedly involved making the subjects' deepest fears and nightmares take some sort of semi-physical form.

The mind control experiments depended on identifying young males with apparent psychic abilities. Many of them came from the original Philadelphia Experiment. The subject would be taken into a subterranean lab and seated in a chair. The chair, referred to as the "Montauk Chair," was specially designed to use a bombardment of radio waves to support the subject's psychic abilities. As the radio waves blasted into the room, the young men who were most psychically talented were able to project creations from their minds into a physical reality, at least briefly.

One of the more colorful tales of the mind control work was that of a young man named Duncan Cameron, who had supposedly also served on the USS *Eldridge*. Cameron was considered to be one of the most talented of the mind-control subjects. He was able to not only make reality change and manifest creations from his mind, but also could alter time. This ability to manipulate temporality created great excitement, and some concern, among the Montauk Project scientists.

As the Montauk Project increased in intensity (and possibly in success), the underground construction continued. Reportedly, the subterranean complex even extended well under the nearby town of Montauk.

As the success with time travel increased, some of the scientists began to feel uncomfortable with the direction of the research. They feared that tampering wantonly with such powerful technology could have catastrophic consequences. They begged the leadership to end the experiments, but were denied. They decided to force the issue. In August 1983, the scientists still in favor of conducting the experiments decided to send test subjects back in time to the USS *Eldridge*, in order to influence that experiment of forty years ago.

The scientists who were seeking to end the Montauk Project seized this opportunity. They used Duncan Cameron to envision a huge Bigfoot-type animal, which then materialized within the laboratory. The enraged beast ran amok, destroying much of the sensitive equipment used to perform the experiments. As the beast obliterated the time travel system, it instantly disappeared. The leadership was in shock over the mayhem. The Montauk Project was ended and the base was abandoned. Those connected with the project were sworn to secrecy.

Rumors abound that some work continues at the base. From the outside, it appears to be completely abandoned, but locals report some comings and goings from the base to this day.

The Town Today

In 2002, the Montauk Air Force Station was renamed its original moniker, Camp Hero, and became part of Camp Hero State Park. Parts of the base remain off-limits, and it is illegal to circumvent the fence. Rumors persist that there are substantial underground structures that were used for the supposed mysterious research.

Directions

From I-495/Long Island Expressway heading east, take Exit 68 toward CR-46/William Floyd Parkway/Shirley/Wading River. In just under 28 miles, turn left onto Route 27. Follow Route 27 through Long Island to Montauk. Turn right onto Camp Hero State Park Road. The radar dish is visible within the park.

NORTH BROTHER ISLAND

This thirteen-acre island was the setting for a documentary on how the world would fare if mankind disappeared. It also was the home of "Typhoid Mary" for several decades.

History

In 1614, two small islands in the East River were named "duo de Gesellen," or "the two companions." What became North Brother Island and the much smaller South Brother Island were left uninhabited for many years. The currents around the islands dissuaded many from traveling to the islands.

The town of Morrisania, which is in the Bronx, purchased North Brother Island in 1871. The Sisters of Charity built a tuberculosis hospital on the island. In 1875, the City of New York bought the island and closed the hospital. In 1885, another hospital, named Riverside Hospital, was built on the island. It was intended to treat infectious diseases, including tuberculosis, smallpox, typhoid, measles, polio, and diphtheria. Access from the mainland was by a ferry, which transported staff and patients from 132nd Street in the Bronx.

Overcrowding was a concern at the hospital, particularly in times of disease outbreaks. During an outbreak of typhoid in the New York City area in 1892, the number of patients exceeded twelve hundred. At times the patients exceeded the number of beds, and tents were used. Heated by wood-burning stoves, several tents caught fire, causing officials to express concern about safety on the island. The death of an infant with measles en route to the island in the winter cold added to the criticism.

North Brother Island was also the site of the most deadly incident in New York City prior to September 11, 2001—the wreck of the *General Slocum*, an excursion steamboat, on June 15, 1904. The ship was carrying more than thirteen hundred passengers, including many children, to a church picnic at Locust Grove on Long Island Sound. What made the accident more tragic were the blunders made before it occurred. Despite huge safety omissions, reportedly corrupt inspectors declared the *General Slocum* seaworthy.

The ship had six lifeboats. They were not only tied down, but also painted firmly to the deck, unusable. The fire hoses on board had rotted, and the lifebelts, which were nailed to the wall among some rusty wiring, were over a decade old. When panicking passengers attempted to use them, many were dragged to the bottom of the river by the weight. The cork within them had disintegrated, and to replace the bulk, iron rods had been inserted into the lifebelts.

The catastrophe began when the ship burst into flames, which could not be extinguished thanks to the frayed fire hoses. The captain, William Van Shaick, attempted to land the ship at the nearest spot to beach the craft. Although he could have made it to Port Morris, in the Bronx, which had piers available, Van Schaick apparently made the decision to head to North Brother Island because Port Morris had flammable wooden docks and oil tanks, making landing there dangerous.

Van Schaick later admitted that he continued facing his ship into the wind, initially hesitant to beach at North Brother, because he feared setting the hospital ablaze. His delay likely increased the carnage, as the wind fanned the flames to an inferno.

Many passengers leaped into the water to escape the flames, but most were unable to swim. Their heavy clothing weighed them down, and multitudes drowned. Others were consumed by the flames on board, or were fatally maimed by the paddle wheel. When Van Schaick finally beached the ship, residents and staff of Riverside Hospital rushed to save lives. Approximately 1,021 passengers died in the tragedy, and only 321 were rescued, including the captain and crew.

Many of the passengers had been from a part of New York City called Kleindeutschland, or Little Germany. At one point, Little Germany was the third-largest German-speaking community in the world. The wreck of the *General Slocum* devastated the community. Almost everyone in the neighborhood had lost a relative or a friend in the disaster. For days, funerals were held every hour to accommodate the many lost. Several community members committed suicide because of the losses they had suffered. Kleindeutschland did not recover from the catastrophe. Following the wreck, many people moved away, and little remains of it today.

Despite proof that officials had bribed inspectors, the Knickerbocker Steamship Company escaped conviction in court, merely paying a small fine. Captain Van Schaick, ultimately, was the only person convicted of a crime. He spent over three years at Sing Sing Prison. In 1912, he was pardoned by President Taft. After his release, he was a broken man and lived out his days in self-imposed isolation. Because of the tragedy, increased oversight on boat inspections was instituted.

By far, the most famous resident of Riverside Hospital was Mary Mallon, also known as Typhoid Mary. Mary Mallon was a housekeeper and cook who was a carrier for typhoid, a bacterial illness that causes very high fever and diarrhea and can be very deadly. As a carrier, Mary spread the illness without becoming affected by it herself.

Between 1900 and 1907, Mary worked as a cook at various venues in Manhattan and Long Island. She passed typhus to hundreds of unwitting diners. As people began to fall ill, she moved on to another employer. The Board of Health questioned her, but she denied being ill, and took no responsibility for spreading the illness. She refused to cooperate with authorities.

Mary Mallon's actions spread typhoid fever to hundreds. Reports of how many deaths she was responsible for vary, with some stating that it was as few as three, others that it was as many as forty-seven. Mary resisted capture, believing herself unfairly persecuted, and managed to evade the authorities. By 1907, the New York City Board of Health had had enough. They declared Mary a public menace and offered her a choice: have her gallbladder removed (this is the organ where typhus lives), or be exiled from the public. She refused the surgery. In Mary Mallon's defense, gallbladder surgery was highly dangerous in 1907.

The Board sentenced her to live in Riverside Hospital for the rest of her life. She was eventually given her own cottage to live in, where she resided with her pet dog. She fought her incarceration and in 1910 was granted a release, with the promise (in writing) that she would not seek employment in the food service industry.

Mary promptly left North Brother Island and adopted a pseudonym, Mrs. Brown. She found employment as a cook at the Sloane Maternity Hospital. Once again, cases of typhoid fever broke out, and authorities traced the outbreak to the cook. It did not take long to discern her true identify.

In 1915, Mary was returned to North Brother Island for the remainder of her life. She was industrious, working at the hospital laboratory during her time there. She suffered a stroke in 1933, and was cared for in Riverside Hospital until her death in 1938.

Riverside Hospital closed shortly after Mary Mallon's death. A tuberculosis pavilion was built in 1943, but was never used for its original purpose. Lack of funding and difficulty finding staff were cited as reasons for its failure. The remaining patients on North Brother Island were removed to other hospitals in the area. However, after World War II, the GI bill, which opened the door for many returning soldiers to attend college, caused a population explosion in the nation's colleges. New York City colleges used buildings on North Brother Island to house their students, who were transported to and from the mainland by ferries from the East 134th Street Terminal.

The city reclaimed the island in the 1950s. A drug rehabilitation center for adolescents was opened in 1952 in the former tuberculosis pavilion. The facility could accommodate one hundred boys and fifty girls. The main concept behind the center was to remove the young people from their detrimental influences and avoid placing them in jails with hardened criminals. Unfortunately, the facility was reportedly poorly run, with corruption running rampant. It was closed in 1963, and the island was abandoned.

The Town Today

Many buildings are still standing on North Brother Island, although their condition is unsafe. Roads, curbs, fire hydrants, streetlights, and other signs of life still poke through the weeds and vines throughout the island. Mary Mallon's cottage no longer stands.

The hospital is still intact. Visitors have noted that the floor of the X-ray room is still littered with film. A theater still stands, but the seats have collapsed. Asbestos is likely in most of the buildings, making them dangerous for visitors. The Nurse's House still stands, as do many of the other original buildings. Others have collapsed. There are holes in the ground where it is possible for visitors to plunge through to basements or utility areas. Extreme caution should be used if visiting this island.

Directions

North Brother Island is between Riker's Island and the Bronx. Access to the site is difficult to obtain. It is illegal to go there without permission. Although it appears very close to the city, and the temptation to simply kayak across may occur to you, this will result in an arrest for trespassing. Rikers Island Prison is nearby, so North Brother Island is patrolled and under surveillance.

If you would like to visit, contact the NYC Department of Parks, which manages the area. The island is home to many birds, including some which are endangered; no visits to the island are permitted from March to October at all, to allow nesting herons to be undisturbed. If you are granted permission, you may charter a boat. No ferry system is currently in place. Few docking options are available on the island.

The buildings on the island are unsafe to enter, for the most part. They are not being maintained, and visitors investigate them at their own significant risk. Beware of hazards throughout the site.

KINGS PARK

Not fitting the typical definition of a ghost town, the former psychiatric center resembled a small city before it was abandoned.

History

For over a century, Kings Park Psychiatric Center cared for mentally ill patients. It now stands empty and abandoned.

During the 1800s, great reforms were made in the care of the mentally ill. Historically, the mentally ill had been treated harshly, in often inhumane conditions. Mental illness was not well understood, and effective treatments were not yet known for most conditions. "Locking them away" was viewed as many families' only recourse when one of their loved ones exhibited symptoms of a mental illness. In large cities like New York City, asylums tended to be dark, overcrowded places, where patients were maintained in depressing, unhealthy conditions. Often, patients deteriorated physically and mentally in these conditions, and few recovered.

In the 1860s, reforms were afoot that would alter the way the public and medical community viewed mental illness. Dorothea Dix, an activist who campaigned on behalf of the impoverished mentally ill, had made an impact on the federal government. Awareness of the inhumane living conditions had appalled the public and an outcry for improvements began.

Thomas Kirkbride, a psychiatrist who advocated for improved treatment of the insane, devised a plan for a system of government-run hospitals for the mentally ill. The Kirkbride Plan was based on the theory of Moral Treatment. Moral Treatment had a compassionate, enlightened focus that encouraged increased human rights for patients with mental illnesses.

The hospitals that Kirkbride envisioned had staggered wings, which improved the amount of available sunlight and fresh air. Patient privacy and comfort were important, and the intent was to work toward curing the patients, instead of simply maintaining their existence.

A series of asylums were built according to the Kirkbride Plan. Many of them were Victorian-style buildings, with large, open grounds. Often, the grounds included working farms, which provided opportunities for the patients to be productive and get exercise.

The Kings Park Lunatic Asylum was a Kirkbride Plan asylum. Owned by the city of Brooklyn and initially named the Kings County Farm, it was built in 1885 on the northern shore of Long Island. It consisted of eight hundred acres with a scattering of various buildings, including living quarters and barns. Although it opened with fifty-five patients in residence, its population grew quickly. Before long, overcrowding became an issue, and concerns about adequate patient care became public. Following protests by the staff and the public, the state of New York took over the facility.

For several years the farm colony became part of the Long Island State Hospital, but eventually became its own entity: the Kings Park State Hospital. The facility grew to encompass over 150 buildings and a staff of almost five hundred. The colony included a laundromat, a library, a furniture repair shop, a bakery, and a recreational facility.

At its peak in 1954, the facility had 9,300 patients. The packed dormitories and never-ending influx of new patients began to erode the bucolic plans of the facility's founders. Farming and fresh air were replaced by pharmaceutical therapies. Electric shock therapy, insulin shock therapy, and lobotomies increased.

The increase in medical interventions decreased the population at Kings Park. Patients who had previously needed to be monitored constantly by staff could now live at home and work in the community, when medicated.

By 1955, the state of New York had come to believe that the system of mental health facilities incurred prohibitive costs. Alternative ways to meet the needs of the patients were found. Kings Park hired social workers to seek alternative placements for many of the patients in community facilities. Elderly patients were transferred to nursing homes. Many patients were prescribed medication and released, but little follow-up care was in place. In 1996, Kings Park Psychiatric Center officially closed, and its remaining patients were transferred to other facilities in the area.

The Town Today

Several buildings still stand within the park. The waterfront area is now known as the Nissequogue River State Park. The rail system that formerly served the center is now a rails-to-trails hiking and biking trail. There are some group homes run on the property, but many of the buildings stand empty and abandoned. It is illegal to enter these buildings. They are state-owned, and trespassers are subject to prosecution. In addition, as with many abandoned structures, it is not safe to enter the buildings.

Directions

From New York City, take Interstate 495 East/Long Island Expressway to exit 42 toward Northern Parkway East toward Hauppauge. Take Exit 45 onto Sunken Parkway North. Take the County Route 11 exit toward Kings Park. CR-11 becomes Old Dock Road Turn right onto St. Johnland Road This road takes you to the Nissequogue River State Park, the waterfront portion of the Kings Park Psychiatric Center.

ROCKLAND LAKE

Before the days of modern refrigeration, a profitable ice business thrived in Rockland Lake.

History

The area that later became known as Rockland Lake was initially settled in 1711 by a man named John Slaughter. Indeed, the early pier and dock were named Slaughter's Landing. At that time, the lake was named Quaspeck Pond, or Quaspeck Lake.

The clear waters of the Hudson River Valley supplied an enormous amount of ice to New York City, which bought almost 300 tons of ice per year. John and Edward Felter and John Perry decided to try an ice business at Quaspeck Lake in 1836. Following a successful run of selling their ice in the city, the men decided to seek some capital. They quickly found seventeen other men with whom to enter into a business. Each of the twenty men invested $100, which was used to build an icehouse and dock.

Some other entrepreneurs began competing with Barmore, Felter, and Company. Eventually the competing businesses united to form the Knickerbocker Ice Company, which became the largest ice supplier in the Hudson Valley. Its yellow ice wagons were a familiar sight in New York City and surrounding areas. The ice from Quaspeck Lake was also shipped across the country, and was renowned for its purity and taste. The Knickerbocker Ice Company promptly changed the name of the lake to Rockland Lake. By 1884, the company employed almost three thousand men. They owned a dozen steamboats and seventy-five ice barges.

While some workers were transient, traveling between the brickyards in the summer and the icehouses in the winter, many others became permanent residents in Rockland Lake, finding summer employment in the local quarry, which was owned by John Mansfield. A town grew to house the workers and their families. Eventually, it encompassed a school, hotels, a post office, two churches (St.

Michaels Roman Catholic church and a Methodist church), taverns, a firehouse, and various stores.

Rockland Lake had a lighthouse in the middle, which functioned until 1923. Built in 1894, the lighthouse quickly began to lean. Before it was replaced by a skeleton tower in 1923, it was found that one side was nine inches lower than the other.

With the introduction of refrigeration, the ice industry became obsolete. The Knickerbocker Ice Company closed in 1924. While some workers moved away in search of jobs, others remained, continuing to work in the quarry, or in the burgeoning hospitality field, catering to wealthy visitors and tourists from NYC. Workers who were tearing down an icehouse in 1926 accidentally set fire to the insulating sawdust. The fire quickly spread to other buildings, eventually burning approximately twelve structures.

The Palisades Interstate Park commission, led by John D. Rockefeller, raised a million dollars to purchase the entire area in 1958. They took over the town, razing most structures and building infrastructure for parkland.

The Town Today

A few remnants of the town of Rockland Lake can still be seen. The firehouse remains, as do a few houses. Most of the structures were demolished, and foundations can still be seen scattered around the area. The walls of Icehouse 3 are still standing, and plans are being made to try to preserve it. Rockland Lake State Park, a 1,079-acre recreational area, offers two swimming pools, golf courses, trails, and tennis courts, as well as boating and fishing.

Directions

From the Palisades Interstate Parkway, take exit 4 toward Route 9W N. Take Route 9W N approximately 9 miles to the park.

Southeastern New York

OLD STONE FORT

A cannonball hole provides an obvious reminder of this building's brave past.

History

The Old Stone Fort in Schoharie has a long and varied history. Built in 1772, it was intended to be a house of worship for the local Reformed Protestant High Dutch Church Society. Reverend Johannes Schuyler was the first officiant, starting his tenure in the pulpit in the summer of 1772.

The many area people who donated materials for the construction of the building were immortalized by having their names carved in the stonework of the church. Some of the names were mysteriously chiseled off at some point in the late 1700s. No one knows why. One theory is that the names of the British Loyalists in the area were removed after the Declaration of Independence was signed.

Another possibility is that the stonecutter removed the names of those who did not pay for his services.

During the Revolutionary War, the Schoharie Valley was subject to raids by the British Tories and their Indian counterparts. In an effort to protect the local citizens, the church was converted into a fort, to provide some safety in the event of a raid. A stockade log fence was built around the building in the fall of 1777. In 1778, blockhouses were built in the northeast and southwest corners of the property, and small shelters were placed within the stockade fence, in the event that local farmers had to seek refuge. Reverend Schuyler died on April 16, 1779, while the church was being used as a fortress. He was buried beneath the pulpit.

Although some small skirmishes were reported, the most serious raid in the area occurred on October 17, 1780. Led by Sir John Johnson, approximately eight hundred Tories and Indians attacked the valley. They burned the farms and crops and drove the locals into the fortress.

Sir John Johnson was a wealthy son of a fur trader and baron, William Johnson. Born in 1741, John Johnson's wish was to get his education and settle down as a wealthy landowner in the Mohawk Valley. The American Revolution derailed his plans. Following the end of the war, he was exiled to British-ruled Quebec. For the rest of his life, he supported British and Indian rights.

The creation of Upper Canada (later to become Ontario) was influenced by John Johnson's support. He died owning enormous tracts of land in both Upper and Lower Canada. Sadly, his burial vault on Mont Saint-Gregoire (formerly Mount Johnson) near Montreal was plowed under in the 1950s, although efforts are under way to restore and preserve the vault.

Johnson was not alone in leading the attack against the Old Stone Fort. He was accompanied by two formidable Indian leaders, Joseph Brant (Thayendanegea) and Cornplanter (Kaintwakon). A Mohawk chief, Brant had attended Moor's Charity School for Indians in Lebanon, Connecticut. He was recognized early for his calm demeanor, intellect, and leadership abilities. He became involved in the

Anglican Church, and was instrumental in translating the prayer book, Gospels, and other important religious documents into Mohawk.

While Brant was a young man, his sister Molly married Sir William Johnson (Sir John Johnson's father). At the age of thirteen, Joseph and his Indian schoolmates followed the elder Johnson into battle during the French and Indian War. Although this early experience with warfare terrified Brant, he went on to become a skilled warrior.

As an adult, Brant was respected not only for his battle skills, but also his quiet leadership and intellect. He was fluent in English and several of the Six Nations Iroquoian languages. Recognizing his value, the British commissioned Brant as a captain in the army. Brant was a tireless advocate for Native American rights, even traveling to England to meet with King George, asking his help in restoring Mohawk lands. He met with the king twice, and a dinner was held in his honor. When asked to bow before the king, Brant famously said, "I bow to no man, for I am considered a prince among my own people. But I will gladly shake your hand."

Cornplanter was a Seneca chief. His wish in life was to live peacefully and tend crops. He had been reluctant to become involved in the Revolutionary War. Like Brant, he feared that if the colonials won the war, the Indians would lose all of their land. He reluctantly aided the British.

Brant, Cornplanter, and Johnson attacked the Old Stone Fort after destroying the nearby farms. A British cannonball tore a hole that can still be seen today in the upper west corner of the building. The siege of the fort was relatively brief. Johnson and his Indian cohorts moved on to attack other towns in the area. With the pacification of the area, the stockade was removed from the fort in 1785. Pews were returned to the building, and it was once again used as a place of worship.

In 1844 the Reformed Society built a new brick church on Main Street in Schoharie. They sold the Old Stone Fort to the State of New York for $800. Company B of the 108th Regiment used the building as an armory until 1868. On June 11, 1873, the New York legislature voted to make the building a historic landmark. In 1888, the

Schoharie County Historical Society, which maintains the Old Stone Fort Museum, was founded.

Many war heroes are buried in the graveyard that completely encircles the Old Stone Fort. One of the most significant graves is that of David Williams. Williams was one of the captors of English spy Major John Andre. John Andre was arrested by Williams and two other men while transporting schematic plans of West Point provided by Benedict Arnold, who was plotting to surrender the fort to the British. David Williams was initially interred elsewhere in Schoharie County, but in 1876, during the celebration of the nation's centennial, his remains were moved to the enclosure of the Old Stone Fort.

The Town Today

The Old Stone Fort Museum is a well-preserved, tourable building. An admission fee is charged to enter the building, but the cemetery can be viewed free of charge. The cannonball hole is easily visible high on the west side of the building. The staff at the fort are friendly and knowledgeable, and many artifacts are housed in the fort—some directly related to the fort, others not. A significant research library is attached to the fort, which contains many historical and genealogical resources.

Directions

On the NY State Thruway, take exit 25A from the east, or Exit 23 from the west. Take I-88 south to Route 30A. Proceed south on Route 30A for approximately 2.75 miles. A hundred yards or so after crossing Fox Creek, turn sharply left at the sign. The fort is located at 145 Fort Road in Schoharie, NY.

NEW LEBANON

Currently in the process of being restored, New Lebanon Shaker Village remains the peaceful, charming location it was many years ago.

History

Like other religious groups before them, the Shakers came to the New World to escape persecution. The Shakers, also known as the United Society of Believers in Christ's Second Coming, originated in Manchester, England, in the mid-1700s, but frequently met with opposition there. They had a tendency to have physical manifestations of religious fervor: They spoke in tongues, shook, shouted, and whirled in fits of spiritual inspiration. Their noisy religious services brought unwelcome attention in England, and the Shakers were accused of disturbing the Sabbath with their enthusiasm.

After coming to America under the leadership of Mother Ann Lee, the Shakers initially settled in Watervliet, New York, but soon spread to other New England and middle Atlantic states. Even in Watervliet, the persecution continued. With tensions between the Americans and British high in the late 1770s, many viewed the Shakers as possible British spies.

Life began to improve for the New York Shakers in 1779, when they attended a Baptist revival near New Lebanon, New York. Not only did the Shakers manifest their expected physical phenomena, but many also experienced emotional and spiritual experiences that caused them to go into trances, writhe on the ground, and shout. Many of the Baptists observing them converted on the spot. The Shaker movement began to gain momentum and further organized itself. The central ministry was located at New Lebanon. The New Lebanon community was founded in 1787, and eventually grew to encompass 6,000 acres, hundreds of buildings, and six hundred members.

While the community was known as New Lebanon, that was actually the name of the town located nearby, so in 1861 the federal government officially changed the Shaker community's name to Mount Lebanon, and gave it its own post office.

The central ministry consisted of two elders and two eldresses. Men and women were considered equals in Shaker society, and governed as such. The Shakers were a rule-governed group. Most aspects of daily life, such as clothing, work, food, daily schedule, worship, and reading material were determined by these rules. Shakers wore a simple uniform, identical to one another, so as to promote unity and not stand out from the rest of the order. By wearing unfashionable clothing, they sought to separate themselves from greed and avarice for fashion and status. Their plain clothing was intended to reflect their modesty.

Their house styles and furnishings likewise were intended to support the society's views on humility and pragmatism. They strove to minimize the decorative touches that many sought to adorn their homes, and instead sought humble, simple items that would not provoke jealousy in others.

The Shakers also believed in celibacy. The idea behind this belief was to free one's spirit from lustful craving. The Shakers believed that humans continued to struggle with the yoke of sin and lust because of Adam's fall from purity in the Garden of Eden. In many other religious groups, the sexes were carefully separated. Not so with the Shakers. The men and women, although sleeping in separate chambers, had many opportunities for contact. Facing and overcoming temptation was viewed as a sign of their commitment to God.

Although there was not a strict segregation between the genders, the Shakers at New Lebanon have rules governing how such interactions might occur. For example, men and women were not to touch, except in medical situations. Women were not allowed to enter male-run shops unchaperoned. Seamstresses were not allowed to work on clothing while a man was wearing it.

When couples gave into the sins of the flesh, it caused great upheaval among the other society members. In some cases, if the guilty parties confessed their sin and repented, they would be readmitted into the society. In other cases, they were removed from the society and exiled. In New Lebanon, for example, Eldress Betsy Bates quickly exiled Theodore Long and Sally Thomas for fornication, sending them in opposite directions from the community before the sin could spread to others. She viewed their sin as a polluting force, to be removed as quickly as possible.

Confession was a basic structure of the Shaker faith. What set Shaker confession apart from other religions' confession was that the members were encouraged to "confess" sins that they had witnessed, but in which they had not participated. Not viewed as tattling, this was a way for the Shakers to keep each others' behavior in check. There was also a type of "whistleblower" protection. The one whose sin was confessed by a witness was not permitted to try to learn the identity of the witness.

New Lebanon, like all Shaker societies, was a neat, clean, orderly place to live. The people worked hard, as laziness was viewed as a sin. Those who shirked their duties or did not shoulder enough of the town's burden were shamed and often did not remain in the community for long. Those industrious souls who stayed were rewarded with lifetime care, room and board, and clothing.

The members of the community either provided a service to the society, such as medicine or cooking, or worked in a business. Being zealous in work was valued among the Shakers. One New Lebanon woman, Tabitha Babbitt, was commended for her ability to knit in the dark, sitting in her bed, without wasting light. The Shakers valued efficiency highly in their work. Non-Shakers often learned new and better building and work techniques from their innovations.

Although the Shakers themselves were celibate, some families joined the society, bringing their children. In other instances, families who had fallen on hard financial times sent their children to be raised by the Shakers. The Shakers viewed this steady stream of young members as the future of the sect, as they did not procreate on their own.

The New Lebanon children attended school seasonally: after harvest for the boys, and during summer for the girls. For the rest of the year, the children worked as apprentices in various businesses and trades.

Although the townspeople worked hard, they did have some enjoyment as well. At times, the Shakers enjoyed sleigh or wagon riding, berry picking, and even swimming. Meals in New Lebanon, like most Shaker villages, were hearty and delicious. At any given meal, a variety of meats, breads, vegetables, desserts, and nonalcoholic beverages were served.

Many of the New Lebanon Shakers lived in the Great House, or Church Family Dwelling, a large multistory building located near the Meetinghouse. The original Great House burned in 1875, and was replaced by the brick Ministry Store Building. Other structures in the village included a tannery (and a tannery pond), a brick shop, a blacksmith shop, two spinning shops, an infirmary, a machine shop, a school (built in 1839), various animal barns, a poorhouse, a dairy, a trustees' office building, and a barn office building.

Buildings were constructed simply and with an emphasis on functionality. The Second Meetinghouse (built in 1824), for example, had an arched roof. It had five entryways: one for brethren, one for sisters, one for elders, and two on the east side for visitors.

In 1793, the ministry approved union meetings, in which society members met, sitting in two rows by gender, facing each other, approximately five feet apart. During these meetings, which were held in the Meetinghouse and lasted an hour, the members were allowed to converse somewhat freely about appropriate topics. The order of seating was managed by the elders and stayed the same, unless illness or death forced changes. The sister often did favors for the brother sitting across from her, such as mending his clothing. The brother reciprocated by helping the sister with tasks more easily done by a male. Children were allowed to attend union meetings, although they were expected to sit quietly and listen, and not to join in the conversation.

Visitors to the community observed that the conversations at union meetings tended toward the mundane. The talk centered on food preparation, crops, animal husbandry, mending clothing, and so on. Once these topics were exhausted, the conversations dwindled. However, this limited scope of conversation at union meetings belied an informed, well-read society. The Shakers of New Lebanon were actually well-informed about events occurring outside their enclave, and subscribed to many periodicals. However, discussion of controversial topics such as politics and literature was discouraged at union meetings.

The union meetings at New Lebanon were a bit controversial, although they continued unchanged for over forty years. Because no private contact was permitted, the meetings were chaste. Some members, however, argued that the relationships formed between certain sisters and brothers mirrored traditional marriage too closely. Some pairings were partnered for many years, and did become very fond of one another. In 1841, possibly because of such concerns, partners were rotated every other week.

The Shakers at New Lebanon took the Sabbath seriously. Although they worked very hard the other six days of the week, at sundown on Saturday, all nonessential work ceased (although animal care continued). On Saturday evenings, special services were held, which were viewed as a time to physically and spiritually end the work week, and to prepare for focus on the worship of God on Sunday.

The Shaker services were, surprisingly, open the public. Again, this was an effort to recruit new members, since the celibate population was unable to provide its own progeny as members. It was also likely that the services were open to the general public in order to dispel persistent rumors that the Shakers danced in the nude and made human sacrifices. The services lasted approximately three hours. The services began with silence. The worshipers rose silently, men and women facing each other, and stood still. In time, some began to tremble and shake. At that point, chanting began, followed by choreographed dancing, with men on one side of the room and women on the other.

Black and white worshipers stood together as equals—an unusual practice at this point in history. Indeed, the Shakers were quite egalitarian when it came to recruiting new members. They were willing to help new members improve and fit in, regardless of their backgrounds. However, if the new members could not, or would not, conform to the society's standards of work ethic, cleanliness, and celibacy, they were asked to leave.

As in all close-knit communities, disease was an ever-present fear. In January, 1813, a measles outbreak killed twenty New Lebanon residents. Children were particularly susceptible to illnesses. Another threat to the community was the often-harsh Berkshire weather. The spring of 1816 was particularly brutal. Every day in May was below freezing. It snowed on June 7 and 8, and the soil was frozen solid on June 9. The Shakers replanted their destroyed crops on June 12, praying that the shortened growing season would be enough for the plants to bear fruit. However, on July 7, the temperature dropped precipitously, and the crops were damaged. On August 23, the Shakers awakened to frost. The following winter was a meager one for the community, and they had to work together to survive until the following spring with their reduced supplies. True to the dedicated community they were, the group indeed made do with what they had until the following spring.

One resident of New Lebanon, Isaac Newton Youngs, from whose diary much of the history of New Lebanon is known, was a master clockmaker. Throughout his life, he made many exemplary timepieces for the various buildings in the community. His main occupation was that of tailor, which kept him very busy, but in his spare time, he made his sought-after clocks. He signed each timepiece and numbered them. In some, he placed a verse about the passage of time. He continued to sign and number his clocks even after 1845, when the Shakers' Millennial Laws of 1845 dictated that no one was to sign or initial items manufactured, so as to remain humble and act as part of a community and not an individual.

The following poem was found within his clock number 23:

Behold! How swift the seasons roll!
Time swiftly flies away!
'Tis blown away as fleety chaff
Upon a windy summer's day.
Then O improve it as it flies
Eternal joys are for the wise.

Five of Brother Youngs's clocks are still in known existence: Three are in the Hancock Shaker Museum, one is in a private collection, and one is Rockford, Illinois, in the Time Museum.

Great changes occurred in 1837. This period in Shaker history became known as the Era of Manifestations. In Watervliet, two young Shaker girls began to have "visions," and appeared to be possessed by some sort of spiritual manifestation. Brother Youngs, a trusted member of the New Lebanon community, visited the community to investigate, and returned to New Lebanon with the belief that the manifestations were real. He reported that the young girls, eyes closed, moved in complete union with one another, sang unfamiliar songs perfectly together in various languages, and appeared to be able to move about without seeing, not bumping into any obstacles.

When Brother Youngs returned to New Lebanon, his neighbors were in awe. As word spread of the phenomenon in Watervliet, so did the number of occurrences of similar manifestations in other Shaker communities. The members in New Lebanon hoped for a similar visitation from the powerful spiritual force. In April 1838, New Lebanon had its wish. Brother Philemon Stewart was overcome with the manifestation of Mother Ann, the original spiritual leader of the Shakers. Speaking with her authority, he exhorted the New Lebanon residents to clean up the site and fix fences, as the disorder of the town offended Mother Ann. The residents quickly moved to satisfy this request. Soon other village members began experiencing visions and other spiritual manifestations.

While the manifestations were welcome, the Shakers realized that this change in their comportment must be managed. They began to try to reserve such manifestations for times when visitors and non-Shaker witnesses were not present. This, of course, suggests that at least some of the episodes were under the control of the person experiencing them. However, some episodes were witnessed by surprised non-Shakers. This was embarrassing to the residents of New Lebanon.

Even weekly Shaker worship began to evolve in light of these manifestations. During services, the worshipers would whirl and turn, and occasionally one would fall to the floor and writhe and contort. Even in regular life, the Shakers sometimes fell to the ground, overcome by the spirit. Nonbeliever workmen and visitors were sometimes alarmed to happen upon a member prostrate on the ground, writhing. Because of this, visitors to the community were barred during the Era of Manifestations, especially from worship services.

In at least one instance, the affected member confessed to pretending to be overcome. This was viewed as fraud by the members, and shook the belief that some of them had in the "gifts." As doubt began to increase among the members, the elders decided to increase policing by reorganizing living arrangements into larger groups. This way there was less privacy, and less opportunity for self-aggrandizing fakery. Many of the members grumbled at having to change their roommates and live in less privacy and comfort, but they agreed. By April of 1841, the Era of Manifestations was over, and the community at New Lebanon again returned to quiet worship. Visitors were again welcomed.

Brother Isaac Youngs, through his descriptions of the "gifts" of the Era of Manifestations, provides some of the most insightful historical knowledge of New Lebanon. His devout spirituality and devotion throughout his life make for a fascinating glimpse into Shaker life and culture. Unfortunately, toward the end of his life, his mental health deteriorated, along with his physical health. Struggling with anxiety and depression, along with a throat ailment that may have been cancer, he fell or leaped from the fourth floor window in the Church Family Dwelling. The Shakers, unlike other Christian sects, did not view suicide as a mortal sin, but rather as a matter between God and the person involved.

New Lebanon continued on for several more decades, but membership dwindled. Communities consolidated as Shaker villages emptied. The last Shakers in New Lebanon left in 1947. A fire in 1972 destroyed the enormous North Family Great Stone Barn, which, at fifty feet wide, two hundred feet long, and four stories high, was the largest stone barn in America when it was built in

1859. The following year the Dwelling House, a five-story, fifty-five-room building, was destroyed to avoid fire or further vandalism.

The Town Today

Although efforts are underway to preserve and maintain what remains of the village, much work remains to be done. Plans are in place to restore the North Family Great Stone Barn and turn it into a museum and visitor center. Other buildings are also being restored. The Meetinghouse, with its arched roof, is still in existence, and is being leased to the Darrow School, a private boarding school. The granary, workshops, and other buildings are still standing and can easily be viewed. As of this writing, entrance to many of the buildings is not possible, but the site is worth a stroll, as you imagine what the quiet, industrious Shaker village must have been like.

Directions

Take Interstate 90 to Exit B3. Turn left on NY Rte 22 toward New Leganon. After approximately 8 miles, turn right onto Route 20. Approximately .3 mile later, turn right onto Shaker Road. Continue up the hill for approximately .7 mile to the site. The address, for GPS units, is 202 Shaker Road, New Lebanon, NY 12125.

SHARON SPRINGS RESORT

This health spa and luxury resort once played host to many illustrious visitors, including Oscar Wilde, Charles Dickens, and Cornelius Vanderbilt.

History

Mohawk Indians were the first to discover the health benefits of the mineral springs at Sharon Springs, a site along the Brimstone River west of Schenectady. Evidence in the form of trail traces, pottery, and arrowheads suggest that the Indians camped nearby, and these natives likely partook in the springs long before the white settlers discovered the healing waters.

The springs that gave the later village its name are dotted throughout the area. The bubbling waters join the Brimstone, which in turn flows into the Mohawk River. The main spring in the town is the White Sulphur Spring; the water bubbling from the earth at this site smells strongly of rotten eggs because of its high sulfur content. The chilly 48-degree water is clear and has no strong taste, unlike many other sulfur springs around the nation.

Sharon Springs rose to prominence in the early- to mid-1800s, an era in which illness was considered a sort of status symbol. Fainting couches were fashionable, and many people carried smelling salts with them. Visiting health-restoring spas was the rage, and the "ill" visitors often brought their family and friends with them and made a holiday of it. The village at Sharon Springs came into existence in 1825, when a man named David Eldridge opened a boardinghouse near the springs. By the mid-1850s, more boardinghouses, along with several large hotels, had been built. Sharon Springs Resort was born.

The natural beauty of the area, along with the landscaping and architectural improvements undertaken by the resort owners, heightened international interest in the region and its health-supporting spas. As word of the health benefits of the springs spread, visitors flooded the area, delighting in the beauty of the backdrop and the luxurious spa treatments available.

Entrepreneurs began to cash in. Beautiful hotels were built, as were numerous guesthouses and bathhouses. The Great House hotel, built in 1836, was purchased by John Gardner and Joseph Landon in 1841 and renamed the Pavilion Hotel. Gardner eventually bought Landon out, and grew the hotel into a beautiful, posh resort on fifty scenic acres. It was fronted by twenty-four enormous Greek Revival pillars—each three stories high—and could house five hundred guests. The Pavilion's veranda was 225 feet long and 21 feet wide, making it was a popular spot for guests to meet and socialize while enjoying the stunning views. The guest register at the Pavilion included such luminaries as Oscar Wilde, the Macy family, Ulysses

S. Grant, Charles Dickens, Whistler's mother, and James Fenimore Cooper.

The nineteenth-century visitors to the springs not only drank the water for its health benefits, but also bathed in it. Ingesting the water was thought to help cure digestive issues and malaria, while bathing was believed to alleviate skin conditions and the symptoms of arthritis. Others breathed in the sulfurous fumes, which were believed to heal lung conditions. The sulfur springs supposedly also had the potential to heal gunshot wounds, rheumatic conditions, gout, and certain types of poisoning.

A "temple" was eventually constructed over the sulfur springs. Early versions of the Sulphur Temple were constructed of wood and were rather simple in design. The current temple, constructed in the Beaux-Arts style, was built in 1927. Still standing, the White Sulphur Temple has eight columns and a detailed ceiling; it formerly had speakers that broadcasted classical music, and chandeliers provided elegant lighting.

Two magnesium springs were located near White Sulphur Spring—one next to the sulfur springs, and the other in a nearby wooded area. People sought out the magnesium springs for their medicinal properties, believed to cure gastrointenstinal ills. The waters served as an antacid and also as a laxative.

The magnesium spring in the woods also had a structure enclosing it, a building known as "Bang's Magnesia Temple." The iron structure was built in 1863 by D. D. Badger of the Architectural Iron Works in New York City. The temple became famous for its elaborate ornamentation and copper roof. Bang's Magnesia Temple was the crown jewel in a complex owned by Henry J. Bang; the resort also included Congress Hall, a large hotel. At its peak, the complex contained the temple, Congress Hall, a lovely bridge over the Brimstone River, bathhouses, ornately landscaped gardens, and a band stage.

Congress Hall competed with the Pavilion Hotel. The hotel's grounds were gorgeous, and its rooms were beautifully appointed. However, despite these amenities, it had difficulty keeping up with the Pavilion. The financial drain was devastating to Bang. An 1875 rumor says that one day, furniture was hastily removed from the hotel; the next day the hotel burned down. Unfortunately, the demise of the Congress Hotel was only one of many eyebrow-raising fires that would destroy a number of the structures in the Sharon Springs resort area.

Another, very different, spring was located near the sulfur spring. The Blue Stone Spring, or Eye Water Spring, contained no sulfur, despite being only a few feet away from the sulfur spring. Instead, the Blue Stone Spring was apparently very effective in treating eye disorders. Evidence suggests that in the 1870s there were three spigots within a stone sink at the Blue Stone Spring. By 1940, many changes had occurred. A bronze lion head covered the spigots, and the stone sink itself was likely encased in cement. The lion's head is no longer at the site, but visitors can continue to use the water from the Blue Stone Spring.

Not far away, to the south of the mineral springs, was the Chalybeate Spring (pronounced ka-leé-bee-at), which was discovered around 1850. This is also referred to at times as the Iron Spring. The water found in this spring was popular for relieving female issues such as menstrual cramps. However, the high iron content in the water was also found to turn women's teeth brown. Despite this unfortunate side effect, the water from the spring was bottled and sold for medicinal purposes.

During the period immediately following the Civil War, it was common for the well-to-do to travel from hotel to hotel and partake in these springs in a sort of "circuit." However, by the beginning of the twentieth century, this mode of spending one's holiday had lessened in popularity. Being ill and needing mineral-water treatments was no longer viewed as fashionable. Wealthy people had started to purchase seaside homes or began visiting resorts in the Adirondacks. During this era, the demographic of the visitors to the Sharon Springs area changed, and the resort became increasingly popular with upper-class Jewish visitors from New York City.

Despite the changes, construction and redevelopment in the town continued. The 1896 Hotel Rosenberg (later renamed Hotel

Roseboro after it merged with the adjacent Howland House in 1900), located on Main Street, appealed to Jewish visitors. Its restaurant served strictly kosher German–Hungarian cuisine and observed the Sabbath. The Hotel Roseboro also had a modern sprinkler system, making it one of the safer lodgings in the area. The hotel closed in the 1960s after a long, successful history.

In 1910 the Chalybeate Spring Temple was built. At one point it was a part of a complex known as Smith's Swimming Pool. The temple itself still stands, although the other buildings of the Smith complex are gone. The temple was turned into a seasonal apartment in the 1960s, and its namesake spring was capped.

Sharon Springs's draw as a resort further declined when a devastating blaze ripped through the area on November 21, 1926. Thirteen buildings burned, including several spa-related businesses and the Sharon Academy Theater, one of the main cultural draws in the village.

The town persevered in the aftermath of the fire, although its days were numbered. The last large hotel to be built in Sharon Springs was the 150-room Adler Hotel, opened in 1929. Like the Hotel Roseboro, it offered fine kosher dining to its visitors, along with medicinal baths, a theater, and many other luxuries. The hotel closed in 1974; the structure, now abandoned, still stands.

During the Great Depression, many hotel owners found themselves unable to make necessary upgrades or pay their creditors, and suspicious fires became fairly common, especially during the "low season" of winter. Besides the possible insurance-gain arsons, several devastating blazes started because dangerous heating sources—candles and oil lamps—were used in the wooden structures throughout the town.

Sharon Springs Resort never truly recovered from the Great Depression and the devastating fires. Efforts were made to change the direction of the resort's attractions, including building a large public swimming pool and opening a ski resort. However, the town never again reached the level of popularity that it had before the turn of the twentieth century. The opening of the New York State Thruway in

1954 funneled travelers away from Route 20 and the town, and its draw as a tourist attraction further waned.

The Town Today

Sharon Springs (population 558) still exists, albeit in a different form. Modern-day visitors can wander among the remaining structures from the spa days, including several of the mineral springs "temples." Maps for self-guided walking or driving tours can be obtained at the Sharon Historical Society and at some businesses in the revitalized village. There are charming shops located in some of the restored historic buildings, along with small art galleries and museums.

The town is also home to Josh Kilmer-Purcell and Brent Ridge, otherwise known as the Beekman Boys. In addition to hosting shows on Planet Green and The Cooking Channel and winning "The Amazing Race," the pair rehabbed the former Roseboro Hotel and opened it as the Beekman 1802 Mercantile. The mercantile sells soaps, cheeses, and other goods produced locally in the Sharon Springs area.

Directions

From Schenectady, take I-88 west. Take Exit 24 toward US-20W/Albany. Follow Route 20W to Sharon Springs. Turn right onto Main Street/Route 10. Parking is available along the street in town. From there, visitors can walk to the historical society's headquarters, located in a small building north of the Roseboro Hotel. Maps of the site and other helpful information are available here, and the remains of the resort are within walking distance.

BANNERMAN ISLAND

While arguably not a true "town," Bannerman Island is a hidden gem for abandonment enthusiasts.

History

Owned initially in the late 1600s by the Philipse family, Bannerman Island was originally named Pollapel Island. Although no one is completely sure where the name came from, one popular theory holds that the name is derived from the Dutch word for "ladle." Young sailors who got drunk or disorderly would be dropped off to sober up on the island. On the ship's return trip, the men would be scooped up in a ladle-type device, and deposited on the ship's deck.

Stories persist about the local Native American tribes believing that the island was haunted. The Indians refused to set foot on the island. The Dutch settlers took advantage of this fear, seeking refuge on the island when the local tribes became hostile.

In December 1900, Francis Bannerman VI purchased Pollapel Island. Bannerman was born in 1851 in Scotland. When he was three years old, his family emigrated to New York City. When his father joined the Union Army during the Civil War, Francis quit school to help support his family. Like his father, Francis made money by retrieving material such as abandoned rope from New York Harbor.

After he returned from the war, Francis's father encouraged him to start his own business, despite the obvious competition to himself. He believed that they would both do better by cornering the market. Following the war, rope was a valuable commodity, in short supply. In 1872, Francis traveled to Ireland to purchase rope. He met his wife, Helen Boyce, there, and married her. They returned to the United States and opened their first store in Brooklyn. Soon they had multiple storefronts, with the business headquarters located at 501 Broadway.

Although Bannerman's business initially focused on produce as well as rope, canvas, and metals, it quickly evolved to become one of the nation's first army-navy surplus stores. Besides military matériel collectors, Bannerman also supplied items to movie production houses, theatrical acts, rodeos, and circuses.

In 1898, at the end of the Spanish-American War, Bannerman purchased a great deal of the surplus American ordnance and matériel.

He moved the items into a warehouse in New York City. His neighbors, however, were not pleased about the huge warehouse full of black powder and other highly combustible materials so close to other buildings and high concentrations of people.

The solution to Bannerman's dilemma was to purchase a small island in the Hudson River, north of the city. He purchased Pollapel Island for $600, plus a three-year $1,000 mortgage. The deed presented to Bannerman forbade him or his descendants from producing alcoholic beverages on the island. Bannerman, who supported Prohibition, readily agreed.

In the spring of 1901, Bannerman started construction of a large arsenal building and a caretaker's house. The arsenal consisted of three floors and was located on the northeast portion of the island. A dock was constructed near the front of the arsenal. The original arsenal was known as No. 1 Arsenal.

Bannerman was a bit eccentric. He designed all of the buildings on the island himself. For some reason, in the original arsenal, he used no right angles at all; the building is shaped more like a parallelogram. Not one to miss an opportunity, Bannerman constructed a large sign that was placed on the side of the arsenal. The sign not only let passengers on ships know about Bannerman's arsenal, but it also told the address of the business headquarters.

Bannerman continued to expand the arsenal, which was soon composed of three storage areas: Arsenals No. 1, No. 2, and No. 3. In 1905, Bannerman began building the castle, the structure most modern visitors associate with the island. The castle was ornate, incorporating Scottish and Spanish influences. By 1909, the castle, now a family home, was largely complete. Bannerman named the impressive building "Crag Inch Lodge," which means "rocky island." The family's coat of arms stood proudly over the large picture window, which showcased a beautiful view of the river.

Bannerman, who liked to have a spot to meditate or rest, placed several areas for relaxing around the island. In addition, he added a ground-floor sun porch to the castle, along with a second-floor "sleeping porch" above. As Bannerman's fortune grew, he added ramparts, a bridge, and twin towers to the island's harbor, and a solitary tower at the south breakwater. He decorated the rampart above his residence with a Civil War cannon, facing southeast toward West Point.

During World War I, the Navy Intelligence Bureau investigated Bannerman and his activities on the island. On April 19, 1918, the island's superintendent, Charles Kovac, was arrested. Kovac had been born in Austria, and his firing of four machine guns to greet passing boats, combined with his nationality, had been deemed suspicious. He and Bannerman were eventually exonerated.

Bannerman died on November 26, 1918, following gallbladder surgery. Many believed that his distress at being investigated impacted his health. Following his death, his wife and sons continued to run the business, storing and shipping ordnance from the island. They discontinued construction, however.

In August 1920, while Helen Bannerman was living on the island, the powder house, loaded with two hundred pounds of black powder, exploded. The explosion was forceful enough to blow a section of the building onto some railroad tracks across the river. The blast could be heard for fifty miles in any direction. Windows in nearby towns shattered. Miraculously, there were no fatalities or serious injuries. This damaging event marked the beginning of the end of Bannerman Island.

After Helen Bannerman died in 1931, her family's visits to the island became less frequent. By 1940, the family unsuccessfully tried to sell the island and the business. In 1957, the business was incorporated. Charles Bannerman, who was in charge by this time, realized that the island location limited the business. Boats were no longer the preferred shipping method: Trucking had replaced them. A new storage facility was built at Blue Point, on Long Island, and the entire business was relocated there.

From the 1960s onward, the island was largely uninhabited. The buildings and dock deteriorated. Harmless relic searchers as well as vandals arrived uninvited on the shores. The damage done to the house and other buildings was heartbreaking to the family.

The island was sold for $108,041 to the Jackson Hole Preserve (a Rockefeller Foundation). The People of the State of New York became the new owners of the island in December 1967. In August 1969, a horrific fire devastated the island. After officials checked for human life, the fire was allowed to burn itself out. When the fire died, only the exterior walls of the castle remained. In 1993, the Bannerman Trust, which included Bannerman family members, was organized to try to preserve the island.

The Town Today

Bannerman Island is open to guided tours. Impressive ruins still stand of the arsenals as well as Bannerman's castle-like home. The home, as of this writing, is being restored, but is not currently open to visitors. The impressive family gardens and grotto may be visited.

Directions

There are two ways to approach Bannerman Island from May through October. One can take a kayak tour through the Bannerman Island Trust. Although pricey, this tour allows more access once on the island. In addition, a great deal of the proceeds are applied toward restoring the island.

A less expensive option is to visit the island by ferry from Newburgh or Beacon. Tickets may be purchased online prior to visiting. The tour guides are very knowledgeable about the island, and permit excellent photography opportunities. Occasional special events are held on the island, some of which are open to the general public.

ACIDALIA

Acidalia, appropriately named for a town whose main industry was the chemical distillation of hardwoods, shares its name with a plain on the planet Mars.

History

Eugene King built a distillation factory in Sullivan County in the 1800s along Basket Brook near Fremont. The factory broke down hardwoods into various chemicals and acids. He named the town that built up around the factory Acidalia, which is a reference to the "Grove of the Nymphs" in Greek mythology. The name is also shared with a large plain on the surface of the planet Mars.

As business improved, King took on a partner, Bert Holcomb. Holcomb was a very well-liked man, exceptionally kind, with a raucous sense of humor. Eugene King himself was respected for being fair, but was described as being a bit difficult to approach because of his stern demeanor.

The Holcomb family had moved to the Fremont/Acidalia area by way of ox-drawn wagon. In the family diary, it was evident that the Holcombs were singularly impressed by the freshness and beauty of the spring water that they found, which would later play a role in the distillation of the area hardwoods. They decided to stay.

The King-Holcomb Company located its factory in that scenic location because of the availability of the wood needed for their chemical processes. Prior to the factory and the town's existence, the forests in the area were incredibly dense. Locals described the woods prior to the factory as spooky and dark, even in the middle of a sunny day.

As the town grew, it eventually became home to a school, a Methodist church, a general store, and a doctor's office. It did not become home to any bars or taverns. Because of his devout Methodist beliefs, King refused to sell or condone liquor in Acidalia. The "dry town" may also have been an effort to improve safety at the factory.

The Holcomb family was reportedly in possession of an old rifle that had been used to murder undersheriff Osman Steele in 1845. Steele was killed during the "Anti-Rent War," which began around 1839 and ended in August of 1845 with Steele's killing. The Anti-Rent War was a form of protest over what farmers viewed as unfair, feudal practices left over from when the Dutch governed New York. The farmers were continuing to pay rents to powerful landowning families, such as the Livingstons, Van Rensselaers, Schuylers, and Hamiltons.

The Anti-Rent War started when the Van Rensselaers, whose patriarch had let the tenants' rent demands lapse as a kindness, attempted to collect the back rents to cover family debts. The farmers, protesting, disguised themselves in wild costumes of calicos, feathers, fur, and sheepskin masks. They earned the name "Calico Indians" from the costumes. Whenever the sheriff appeared at a farm to collect the rents, the Calico Indians would surround him on horseback. They disarmed the sheriff and sent him on his way. It was generally viewed as harmless and mischievous, as opposed to seriously dangerous.

On a few occasions, the sheriff managed to abscond with livestock as rent payments. The Calico Indians retaliated by using snipers to kill the sheep and cattle before they could be sold. At their most mischievous, they kidnapped sheriffs and took them to a local tavern, holding them prisoner until they finally agreed to jump up and down and shout, "Down with rent!" before being released.

The Anti-Rent War came to a violent head in August 1845, when Sheriff Green More and his undersheriff and jailer, Osman Steele, approached Moses Earle's farm near Andes. The Calico Indians surrounded the lawmen, blowing horns and shouting. Mr. Steele resisted the "Indians," and they shot him three times. He died later that same day. His death turned public attention against the Calico Indians and their anti-rent views. The Calico Indians quickly disbanded. Many turned the costumes into curtains and blankets. Many arrests were made in the case of Steele's death, and eighty-four men were convicted. Two men were hanged for the crime, and thirteen served prison terms. In 1846, John Young, the newly elected governor, pardoned all Calico Indians remaining in jail, and in 1848, the New York legislature abolished the antiquated rent system. It is unclear what happened to the rifle in the Holcombs' possession, but it was considered to be an important historical artifact.

Acidalia was a charming town during its existence. Besides other aspects of small-town life, it also boasted a talented baseball team, called the McAdams' Team. It was named for the fact that many of the team members had that surname, as it was a common name in the area.

Eventually, the clear-cutting practices of the King-Holcomb Company decimated the forests around Acidalia. In addition, during World War I the chemicals produced in Acidalia began to be synthesized from petroleum, rendering the King-Holcomb Company obsolete. When the factory closed, the families began to move away. Today, little remains to mark the once-prosperous town.

The Town Today

Little remains of Acidalia. There are some foundations scattered around the valley.

Directions

From Binghamton, NY, take Route 17E. Take exit 87 to Route 97, toward Hancock. Pass Hancock, and continue on Route 97. Turn left onto CR-94. When you reach Fremont, turn left onto Route 95/Hankins Road. The site of the town is approximately .5 mile past Fremont.

TRAPP MOUNTAIN HAMLET

The remains of this once-busy village are located in a beautiful natural area that is popular with hikers.

History

Historians have located artifacts and other proof that the area where Trapp Mountain Hamlet was located has been inhabited for as long as 10,500 years. Evidence of Paleo-Indian cave shelters nearby have spurred additional research into the rich past of the area. In more recent times, the village was a busy community of approximately sixty homes. The area was first settled in the 1700s, when Dutch settlers and several English families moved to the area.

At its height, the town contained a chapel, a general store, a tavern, a school, two mills, and cemeteries. A one-room school was built in 1850. Members of the community typically worked as woodcutters, shaved barrel hoops, or picked berries. Others worked in nearby hotels. The first of these mountain hotels was built in 1859 by John Stokes at Mohonk Lake, not far from Trapps. He later built two others at Minnewaska Lake.

Subsistence farming was common in Trapp, but the rocky soil was not conducive to larger, more productive farms. The local villagers often planted small crops of corn, rye, oats, or potatoes. They sometimes kept a few farm animals for the use of the immediate family. Some of the residents sold extra butter, fruit, and eggs to supplement their income.

Berry picking was a lucrative industry for Trapps. From July through September, the residents took to the woods, picking thousands of buckets of huckleberries. At times the locals set the woods on fire to stimulate the growth of the berry bushes.

Around the time of the Civil War, Trapps reached its highest population. However, by the 1920s, the number of residents had declined significantly. In the early 1900s, technological advances began to eliminate some of the mountain industries that the locals depended upon. Steel hoops replaced wooden barrel hoops, and the need for millstones disappeared. Residents of Trapp began to struggle economically, and some moved away. When the Spanish Flu raged through the area in 1918, it took an additional toll. Many of the residents moved to the nearby towns of New Paltz and Ellenville.

The one remaining cabin in the town belonged to Eli and Anna Van Leuven, who were woodcutters. They earned a living cutting firewood for a hotel that stood in nearby Minnewaska State Park, supplementing their income through subsistence farming, making charcoal, and collecting tolls on the Wawarsing/New Paltz Turnpike, which was the first major road built over the Shawangunk Ridge. Mr. Van Leuven lived in the house, which had no running water or electricity, until his death in 1956. With his death, Trapps was officially a ghost town.

The Town Today

As mentioned before, the Van Leuven cabin still stands. Although it was previously used as overnight lodging for hikers, it is now open to the public as an interpretive center. There are knowledgeable historians on site to explain the area. In addition, there is an audio walking tour of the area.

There are many foundations and basement holes left behind from the town. Following the West Trapps Trail, visitors can see the abandoned millstone quarry, bridge foundations, the stone wall that marked the Fowler family property line, and the Fowler family cemetery. Ben Fowler, the patriarch, and his family are buried there. The earliest marked grave is from 1866. Following the path past the cemetery, visitors can find the Van Leuven Cabin.

Other signs from the town can be seen if you drive west along US Route 44/45, past the West Trapps Trail. Turn right onto Clove Road to the Coxing Trailhead. From there, visitors can see the foundations of the former Enderly sawmill and farm, as well as the Enderly cemetery.

Directions

Take the New Paltz exit, Exit 18, off of the NYS Thruway. Go 7 miles west on Route 299, through New Paltz, to the end. Turn right on Route 44-55. The Preserve Visitor Center will be in .5 mile, on your right. Go 1.3 miles past the visitor center and turn right into the parking area. This parking area reportedly fills quickly with hikers on peak weekends. Trail maps can be found online and at the visitor center.

CANNONSVILLE

You need a scuba tank and flippers to visit this beloved town, which was submerged to create a watershed for New York City.

History

Cannonsville's history began in 1786, when a young man named Jesse Dickinson purchased land belonging to Colonel Bradstreet. He ventured up the Delaware to see his purchase and was thrilled by its beauty. He laid out a city there, naming it Dickinson City. He returned to Philadelphia to recruit investors to help him carry out his plan, and had little difficulty finding others who shared his enthusiasm. He brought men and materials back up the river, and built a gristmill and a hotel, which he named "City Hall." City Hall later served as a schoolhouse. It stood near the bank of the Delaware River where Trout Creek entered it.

Despite the amount of building and developing that Dickinson did, he ultimately failed in business. He sold a section of his land to Wait Cannon, from Sharon, Connecticut, in 1796. The town got its name from Cannon's son, Benjamin Cannon, who was also the first postmaster there.

The men who came with Jesse Dickinson brought their families to the wilderness, and made up the early population of the area. The men built the original sawmill on the Delaware River, but because the low elevation of the area they chose on the river did not allow for a fast turn of the mill, it was nicknamed "Slow and Easy Mill." Another mill was built a mile and a half upriver. The second mill had much faster-running water, and was named "Speedwell." The mountain west of the mill took its name from the mill.

Jonas Parks was one of the residents of Cannonsville, as it came to be named. There was a significant salt lick located on the hillside near his farm. One night he was walking home and he thought heard something breathing behind him as he passed the salt lick. He assumed that it was a deer, as deer occasionally followed him from the salt lick. He had his gun with him, as usual, and he fired into the dark in the direction of the sound. He returned the next morning and found that he had shot a large mountain lion, likely saving his life.

Calvin Chamberlain, originally from Vermont, was another resident of the town. He held the area's first Sunday School in his home, and it is said that after the lesson, he read the newspaper to the children. He was also an abolitionist, and his home was part of the Underground Railroad for escaped slaves.

The area was relatively untouched by the ravages and massacres of the French and Indian War and the Revolutionary War. The peaceful history brought more settlers to the area, and the town grew. Besides the lumber mills, gristmills were built, dairy farms became prominent, and businesses such as blacksmiths, harness shops, cobblers, and cooperages appeared.

Cannonsville became home to several churches that served the religious needs of the residents. In 1830, a branch of the Deposit Baptist Church was begun with fifteen members. By the end of September, 1831, they had fifty members, and became their own entity: The Cannonsville Baptist Church. The church meetings were held in schoolhouses around the area until 1852, when the members bought a former schoolhouse for their use.

For the next ten years the congregation used the schoolhouse, intending to build their own church when funds permitted. A local man named Canfield Boyd had been carefully cutting and preparing lumber for the new home he was going to build, as his expanding family was outgrowing their small home. However, he decided to donate all of the lumber for the building of the church, which he believed was more important than his home. It was many years before the Boyd family were able to produce enough lumber to finally build their own home. On June 17, 1868, a church sixty feet by forty feet was dedicated, and a parsonage was quickly built adjacent to it.

The Methodist Church was organized around 1830. Few records of this church remain. The Presbyterians met in the Cannonsville Schoolhouse, and were known for some time as the Second Presbyterian Society of the Town of Tompkins. In 1935, the Methodist and Presbyterian churches joined together to form the United Church of Cannonsville, which held services until 1955.

In one of the more exciting events in the town's history, a driver and fine team of horses were pulling a full load of lumber across the town's covered bridges one rainy day in 1900. Perhaps due to the rain, the bridge collapsed with the wagon on it. A dramatic rescue ensued. The driver survived, but the team of horses was swept downstream and drowned.

The much-loved town eventually came to an end when the government decided that a large reservoir was needed to provide water for New York City. The townspeople were bought out over the decade of 1955 until 1965. The reservoir covered 19,900 acres in Delaware County, taking almost a hundred farms and displacing almost a thousand people from Cannonsville. Cemeteries were emptied and bodies were interred elsewhere. Water filled the valley in 1966, and Cannonsville was no more. The reservoir is approximately fifteen miles long and a half mile wide.

The Town Today

The remains of the town are completely submerged by the Cannonsville Reservoir.

Directions

From Binghamton, take Route 17 East. Take the exit for Route 8/ Route 10 (Exit 84). Turn right on Buck Road. These directions will take you to the Cannonsville Reservoir.

Northeastern New York

FORT TICONDEROGA

This remote outpost was only active for a few decades, but its importance in the early years of the nation is unmistakable.

History

In the 1600s and 1700s, waterways were the only reasonable, convenient mode of travel through the New York area. Controlling the region's waterways was critical. Ticonderoga's location made it valuable to the various powerful nations with interests in the region.

In 1609, the French explorer Samuel de Champlain was the first white man to visit the site of Ticonderoga. Traveling with a war party consisting of Huron and Montagnais Indians, Champlain entered the large lake that would later bear his name one evening in late July. In the darkness, the party realized that they had stumbled upon a large opposing war party of Iroquois at the Ticonderoga peninsula. The Iroquois quickly beached their elm-bark canoes on the peninsula and hastily built a crude stockade of tree logs and branches. The two groups of Indians, carefully just out of each other's arrow range, traded taunts and insults throughout the night.

The next morning the battle began. The Huron shielded Champlain and his comrades from the view of their enemies at first, and the Iroquois expected an easy victory over the badly outnumbered Canadian Indians. Suddenly, the Huron parted, allowing the Iroquois their first-ever view of a white man. This sight alone was enough to shock the Iroquois, giving the Huron a momentary advantage. And the Iroquois were completely unprepared for Champlain's arquebus, an early muzzle-loaded gun. Champlain raised the gun and fired, killing two Iroquois leaders and one warrior in one lucky shot. After a second shot, the Iroquois turned and fled, pursued by the Huron.

That night, the celebrating victors chose one of their two Iroquois prisoners to torture. Champlain tried at first to ignore the screams of agony from the victim but was eventually driven to ask for the Hurons to stop their torment. They refused. Champlain stepped forward with his arquebus and shot the Iroquois prisoner in the head to end his misery. The Hurons then cut out the Iroquois' heart and tried, unsuccessfully, to force the other prisoner to eat it. The group then returned to Canada, and no white people returned to Ticonderoga for some time.

Following Champlain's devastating victory over the Iroquois at Ticonderoga, the Iroquois were cautious about attacking the French. They did not forgive, however, and planned their revenge. They began allying themselves with the Dutch, trading furs for muskets. In the summer of 1641, hostilities broke out between the Hurons and their French allies, and the vengeful Iroquois.

The French decided to build a fort at Ticonderoga as the hostilities increased. Canadian governor Vaudreuil requested that military engineer Michel Eustace Gaspard, Marquis de Lotbinière, build the fort to protect the French claim to the strategic portage between Lake Champlain and Lake George. A fort would help to cement the French claim to the entire region.

Lotbinière was young, with no real building experience. However, his family was well connected and wealthy. His connections allowed him to work by his own rules, more or less. He traveled to the site to begin the fort, to be named Fort Carillon, in September 1755. As a reward for his service to France, he was awarded two large tracts of land in the area of Ticonderoga.

As Lotbinière began construction on the fort, cold weather set in. By December, work slowed to a stop. By then, there were approximately four hundred men in residence, living in the four newly constructed barracks and twenty huts. Before the worst weather hit, the fort walls were several feet high. Twelve cannons and numerous small weapons were already on site. By the summer of 1756, the four bastions of Fort Carillon were seven feet high, and more than thirty cannons were in commission.

The new field commander, Louis Joseph, Marquis de Montcalm, left to wage a successful campaign against Fort Oswego. He expected to return to a nearly completed Fort Carillon. Instead, when he returned with his chief aide, the brilliant lawyer Bougainville (who later introduced the bougainvillea flower to Europe from the South Seas), he was frustrated with the slow progress. Montcalm and Bougainville blamed Lotbinière.

One issue that concerned Montcalm was the location of the fort. Lotbinière had not located it optimally. The site did not allow for effective command of the narrows, and was too far inland for accurate weapons fire. Because of this, Montcalm ordered a second, smaller fort, called a redoubt, to be built on the tip of the peninsula. The redoubt was initially built rather crudely, with logs and dirt, but was later rebuilt with stone.

The other concern that Montcalm and Bougainville had was that the fort that Lotbinière was building was approximately half the size it should have been. Compared to the other forts being built by the British in the area, Fort Carillon appeared to be too small to mount an effective defense. Bougainville believed that Lotbinière was relying on his powerful relatives to smooth over his poor work practices.

Lotbinière also controlled all of the commodities at the fort, including wine and candles. He issued the soldiers and workers his own "currency," which they then spent at his canteen. At times, apparently because of poor planning on Lotbinière's part, the wine, oil, and candles at the canteen ran out, which infuriated Bougainville. The leaders began to suspect that it was not in Lotbinière's best interest to ever complete the fort's construction.

When winter came and the fort was still not complete, Montcalm ordered the weaker sections to be fortified with vertical logs, to ward off invasion. Two hundred men were left at the fort for the winter, while the others, along with Montcalm and Bougainville, returned to Montreal.

The first serious attack on Fort Carillon came in July of 1758. British general James Abercromby attempted to send several cannons down river by barge in an attempt to prepare to attack the French left flank. He was unsuccessful. Carillon's cannons sank two of the barges, and forced the others to turn back.

The British attack was poorly coordinated, with Abercromby's troops advancing in thin, single lines, rather than in a concentrated attack, which historians believe might have been successful. The battle lasted approximately six hours. In the end, even though the British outnumbered them by four to one, the French prevailed. Two thousand British troops were killed, including approximately five hundred members of the Black Watch, the legendary 42nd Highlanders. The French lost 377 men. Montcalm later had a large wooden cross erected at the center of the main area his troops had defended. It was blessed by Abbé Piquet. A replica of the cross now stands at the entrance to Fort Carillon.

In 1759, troops under General Jeffrey Amherst attacked Fort Carillon. Although the fort had been strengthened structurally following the Abercromby attack, the other skirmishes throughout New France had left the fort understaffed and undersupplied. In addition, Amherst was much better prepared than Abercromby had been. The British, approaching on the morning of July 23, found the French main line unmanned. Astounded, Amherst quickly set up the British front line at this wall and began building firing platforms.

Amherst laid siege to Fort Carillon, blocking reinforcements or supplies from reaching the French. The French fired heavily on the British, with little effect. Amherst lost few men and used his weaponry sparingly. The siege was over by July 26. The French surrendered, but only after apparently lighting a slow fuse that blew up the powder magazine. The British held control of the burning Fort Carillon, which they promptly renamed Fort Ticonderoga.

The fire from the French sabotage of the fort burned for days, destroying most wooden parts of the structure. The British tried desperately to quench the fire with a bucket brigade, with little success. However, when the fire died, the victors found that little actual structural damage had been done. The British left a small contingent behind and turned their attention elsewhere.

The war moved on. Canada fell to the British, and the need for forts on Lakes Champlain and George was greatly diminished. However, the British continued to maintain a minimal presence at Fort Ticonderoga and Fort Crown Point. The commanders of these forts, with little to occupy their time, focused on farming and animal husbandry.

In 1773, a severe fire destroyed much of Fort Crown Point, leaving Fort Ticonderoga as the lone significant force on Lake Champlain. By the spring of 1775, the fort was falling into a derelict state. It was manned by forty-two soldiers, half of whom were elderly or incapacitated in some way. The meager garrison was led by Captain William Delaplace.

On April 19, 1775, the American Revolution began in the tiny town of Lexington, Massachusetts. The American colonials rushed to arm themselves against the powerful British army. Benedict Arnold, then a captain in the continental army, was aware of the substantial weaponry housed at Fort Ticonderoga. On May 3, 1775, Arnold was given permission by the American government to raise a company of four hundred men to try to take the fort.

Interestingly, Arnold's commission was issued by a British spy, Dr. Benjamin Church. It is a mystery why Church did not warn Delaplace, the leader of the garrison at Ticonderoga, of the impending attack. It is likely that the answer is simply that Church's communications traveled slowly because they had to take secret, circuitous routes to their targets. In any case, Church did not notify the British in time about the planned invasion.

As the colonial troops marched north, they paused in Bennington, Vermont. At the same time, Ethan Allen and the Green Mountain Boys were meeting at the Catamount Tavern (known for its stuffed mountain lion placed atop a pole snarling in the direction of New York), discussing a similar plot. The two groups decided to team up. However, the Vermont militiamen were unwilling to accept now-colonel Benedict Arnold as their leader, choosing Ethan Allen instead. Eventually, Allen agreed to lead jointly with the outraged Arnold.

Allen was sent ahead to scout the fort, and others were sent to kidnap Major Philip Skene, a local Tory landholder. They hoped to commandeer Skene's boats for transport across the lake. Unfortunately, Skene did not have the boats they had expected. Near dawn on May 10, a few small boats were found, and the colonials began ferrying men across the lake. As light began to grow, only eighty men had made it across, but Allen and his men could wait no longer. They approached the fort.

A British sentry spotted them and attempted to fire upon them. His weapon jammed. The sentry fled without alerting the rest of the fort. The Green Mountain Boys raced up the steps and into the fort, waking the British soldiers in the barracks. Demanding to be taken to Delaplace, Allen shouted, "Come out, you old rat!" Delaplace's second-in-command appeared, carrying his breeches. Threats ensued until Delaplace himself appeared. He demanded to know under what authority the attackers were acting. Ethan Allen reportedly replied, "In the name of the Great Jehovah and the Continental Congress!"

Ticonderoga passed into colonial hands with no bloodshed. This was viewed as America's first major victory in the Revolutionary War.

The remaining colonials were ferried across to the fort, and looting commenced. Benedict Arnold, whose training as a soldier emphasized discipline, attempted to intervene, with little success. Reportedly, a few sneaky gunshots were aimed at Arnold, but they missed.

Benedict Arnold recognized the importance of controlling the new nation's waterways. As his own men finally crossed the lake to join him, he set about securing the ships and arming them for possible battle. By May 22, Arnold was firmly in control of Ticonderoga, and Ethan Allen and the Green Mountain Boys had begun returning to Vermont. Arnold controlled Crown Point and Ticonderoga, effectively commanding the entire lake. He had also created the first American navy.

Arnold moved on to other battles, and command of the lake forts fell to General Philip Schuyler. In late 1775, Henry Knox was ordered to travel to Ticonderoga and return with any usable cannons to help defend Boston. Using boats and, later, heavy sleds and oxen, Knox moved an enormous load of cannons and mortars out of Ticonderoga, across the lake, and over land, despite the hardships of ice and blizzards.

During this period, poor provisions and illnesses such as smallpox took a toll on the fort. Colonel Anthony Wayne, of Pennsylvania, wrote, "(Ticonderoga) appears to have been the last part of the world that God made and I have some ground to believe it was finished in the dark . . . I believe it to be the ancient Golgotha or place of skulls—they are so plenty here that our people for want of other vessels drink out of them whilst the soldiers make tent pins of the shin and thigh bones of Abercrombies [*sic*] men."

In July 1776, the Americans officially decided to refortify Ticonderoga and Mount Independence, which was on the east side of the lake. Soldiers were better fed, illness decreased, work on fortifications increased, and soldiers began to drill again. However, by winter, conditions had again deteriorated. The men shivered in tents as blizzards raged, and the sick and dying lay among corpses in the fort's "hospital," with no beds or bedding. By mid-February, Wayne's Pennsylvania soldiers had had enough, and threatened to mutiny.

The uprising was quelled, but General Wayne was grateful for the coming of spring. Wayne left for Valley Forge not long after.

In June 1777, British general John Burgoyne marched south from Canada, intent on taking Albany. Determined to take Fort Ticonderoga first, he approached with huge cannons. First, his men torched the sawmills near the fort, and on July 2 they set fire to the defensive works and the unprotected watercraft on the lake.

General St. Clair, the commander of the fort, attempted to hold his defenses against the British. When the Americans realized the scope of the massive, well-armed forces they were facing, they prepared for the worst. Their fears were realized on July 5, when they observed the British setting up cannons on Mount Defiance, which would have sealed Ticonderoga's doom. The Americans hastily retreated. Following the American abandonment, Ticonderoga was lightly manned by the British. Burgoyne and much of his force moved on, ultimately to surrender at Saratoga.

Colonel John Brown returned to the area in September, with the intent of releasing the American prisoners held at the fort. However, he was also under orders to carry out an actual attack on the fort if the opportunity presented itself. Brown successfully retook Mount Defiance and the blockhouse that the British were building, and likewise released the American prisoners from a barn near Lake George. He was unsuccessful in attacking the fort, and retreated.

As the Revolutionary War came to a close, the British retreated, burning the fort as they left. Over a hundred years later, efforts to rebuild and restore the fort began, leading to its current state as a popular tourist destination.

The Town Today

The remaining historic portions of Fort Ticonderoga have been lovingly restored, while the rest has been re-created. The grounds are extensive and fascinating. There are interpreters and docents available throughout the property to demonstrate period activities or to answer questions. A gift shop and snack bar are available. There is an admission charge ($17.50 for an adult at the time of this writing).

The fort is open from mid-May to mid-October from 9:30 A.M. to 5 P.M. daily.

Directions

From US Interstate 87 (North or South), take Exit 28 onto NY Routes 22 and 74 East. Follow for approximately 18 miles. Turn left onto Route 74 East. Follow Route 74 East for approximately .5 mile. The entrance to Fort Ticonderoga is on the right.

ADIRONDAK/TAHAWUS

A classic ghost town, complete with decaying buildings disappearing into the forests, Tahawus is worth the trip to visit.

History

Archibald McIntyre, who built the Elba Iron Works near Lake Placid, was responsible for building up the town of Tahawus. McIntyre was born in Scotland in 1772. His parents emigrated to then-British-controlled America in 1774. McIntyre's family survived the American Revolution, settling in Albany, where Archibald grew to be a surveyor and schoolteacher.

An ambitious young man, McIntyre became a member of the state assembly in 1798, and then became state comptroller in 1806. Unfortunately, he lost his post after fifteen years because of his accusation that the governor, Daniel Tompkins, had "misplaced" $120,000 of the state's funds. While in politics, McIntyre also sought his fortune in business. In particular, he was interested in exploiting the iron ore in the Adirondack region for use in producing needed metals for the growing United States.

The Elba Iron Works eventually failed, in part because of issues with the quality of the ore, and in part because of the difficulty of getting the products to market. Another major reason that the business failed was that the summer (or lack thereof) of 1816 was the final straw for the struggling townspeople.

The summer of 1816 was apparently impacted by the accumulated ash from several distant volcanoes erupting and spewing ash into the air, blocking out the sun. That summer was brutally cold, with snow in June, frozen ground in July, and frost in August. Crops, critical for survival, failed, and people were suffering and starving. Many left the area. In 1817, McIntyre closed the Elba Iron Works.

In October 1826, an Indian scout named Lewis Elijah Benedict approached David Henderson, one of McIntyre's associates. Benedict was the son of Sabael Benedict, a well-known Penobscot Indian who was the first settler in what is now Hamilton County. In fact, the village of Sabael is named for him, as is the gorgeous Indian Lake. Lewis Benedict was a trapper, and therefore was very familiar with the local mountains and forests.

Henderson told Benedict that he hoped to find a lost silver mine in the area. Benedict was unable to help with silver, but reached into his pocket and instead pulled out a piece of iron ore. Henderson was a bit disappointed, since the McIntyre mines in Elba had not proven to be successful, and silver was likely to be much more lucrative. However, he was a businessman and unwilling to turn down a prospect. He paid Benedict $1.50 and a plug of tobacco to lead him through Adirondack Pass, later renamed Indian Pass.

When Benedict led Henderson to the seam of ore, Henderson was impressed. The vein was 50 to 80 feet wide, and miles long. Henderson returned to McIntyre with the information. McIntyre immediately purchased all the land that he could buy, eventually totaling 105,000 acres. Because of the remoteness of the area, it took six years to set up the iron forge and mining operation. But by 1832, the town of McIntyre was born to house the various mine workers. The name was changed to Adirondak in 1848, when the federal government granted the town its own post office.

By 1834, the iron forge at Adirondak was producing fifteen hundred pounds of iron ore per week. Unfortunately, getting that product to market proved to be an insurmountable task. The existing roads were meager and in poor shape, and no rail service was available yet. As McIntyre wrote to an associate, "We are at least a half century too early in opening that region."

By 1836, McIntyre had given up, and the miners had moved away. In 1837, David Henderson, now McIntyre's son-in-law, took over the business in Adirondak. Briefly successful, the business soon foundered again because of the ever-present difficulty of getting the products out of the mountains.

On September 3, 1845, Henderson, his son, and their guide John Cheney were scouting for water sources to divert past the furnaces. They spotted some ducks on a pond. Henderson handed his gun to Cheney to shoot the ducks, but Cheney was unable to get a clean shot. He handed the still-loaded gun back to Henderson, who placed it back in his backpack. When he set the backpack on a rock a short time later, the gun went off, fatally wounding Henderson. A monument stands on the site, which was renamed Calamity Pond.

In 1854, a new blast furnace was built a half mile away from the original furnace, in an attempt to lure potential buyers. At that time, sixteen homes remained in Adirondak, along with a company store, a large boardinghouse, and a combination church and school.

Unfortunately, the plan failed. Buyers failed to materialize, and a terrible flood damaged the operation in 1856. McIntyre's death in 1858 spelled the official demise of Adirondak as well. Everyone moved away, leaving only Robert and Sarah Hunter, who were paid a dollar a day to remain and watch over the site. The town became known as "the deserted village" in travel brochures. After Sarah Hunter's death in 1872, the site was again deserted. In fact, she was the last addition to the Adirondak cemetery, which is located in the woods between the town and Henderson Lake.

After the Hunters were gone, the town began to deteriorate in earnest. However, in 1876, McIntyre's heirs had the idea to turn the 105,000-acre tract into an exclusive hunting club. The Adirondak Club was opened. In 1898, it was renamed the Tahawus Club. Although the hunting club initially used the miners' homes as a camp, in the early 1900s the club began tearing down some of the more rustic structures and adding some new buildings.

On September 6, 1901, President McKinley was shot while attending the Pan-American Exposition in Buffalo. He appeared to be recovering well enough that his vice president, Theodore Roosevelt, felt comfortable accepting an invitation to go hunting at the Tahawus Club as a guest of James McNaughton, then the president of the club. Unfortunately, McKinley took a turn for the worse, and messengers were sent to find Roosevelt. It was not an easy task. One of the hunting club guides frantically searched Mount Marcy until Roosevelt was found. David Hunter, the son of the former caretaker, rushed Roosevelt by carriage late on Friday, September 13, 1901, on the first leg of his trip to Buffalo to succeed McKinley.

In the 1940s, a different mining company set up business near the Tahawus Club. The new company, the National Lead Company, sought to extract titanium from the generous Tahawus Tract to use in paint for warships during World War II. During this period, the titanium mine families lived in the remaining Adirondak miners' homes, near the Upper Works. Following the conclusion of the war, mining again tapered off at the site. By 1963, the National Lead Company declared that it was no longer interested in being a landlord, and ended any occupation at the site. The Tahawus Club relocated nearby, where it remains today. Adirondak/Tahawus officially became a ghost town.

The Town Today

Adirondak/Tahawus is an exciting ghost town to visit. There are several houses, many caving in, along Route 25. They are not safe to enter, and visitors should use great caution when exploring. Going into the woods reveals even more empty houses, in various stages of decay. The mine is not open to the public and is behind a fence. Permission must be obtained before entering.

Directions

From Newcomb, NY, take Route 64 (Blue Ridge Road) east. Turn left on Route 25. There is a sign for Tahawus at the intersection. Follow this road to the end. On the way, you will pass the iron forge on your right, which is worth a visit. At the end of Route 25, there is a trail-head and parking lot. The ghost town is scattered around this site.

FORT CROWN POINT

Not far from Fort Ticonderoga, Fort Crown Point shared the more famous fort's role of being the key to the continent.

History

Crown Point, which is located at a narrow point in Lake Champlain, was named Pointe à la Chevelure, or Scalp Point, by the French. At different points during its existence, it was controlled by the French, the British, and the Americans. During the French and Indian War, the French recognized that Lake Champlain would provide an easy route to transport goods and soldiers. The land that became Fort Crown Point was perfectly situated to control that route.

Fort Crown Point's history actually started much earlier, however. In 1690, French and Indians used the peninsula of land that would later be the site of Crown Point as a staging area for attacks on the British in Schenectady. The British, planning retaliation, sent Captain Jacobus deWarm to determine the strength of the French army. DeWarm built a small fortress across the narrows from Crown Point, on what is now Chimney Point, Vermont. Peter Schuyler, a British commander, used the Crown Point peninsula to facilitate his attack on La Prairie, which was just south of Montreal.

In 1713, at the conclusion of Queen Anne's War, also known as the War of Spanish Succession, the Treaty of Utrecht was signed. The treaty designated Split Rock, located almost twenty miles north of Crown Point, as the boundary line between British and French lands.

The French disputed the Treaty of Utrecht's boundary. In 1730, they built a small stockade at Chimney Point, which enraged the British. With the small wooden stockade in place, France began to plan for a more substantial occupation of the area.

Chaussegros de Lery, an engineer, designed the French fort at Crown Point (or Pointe à la Chevelure, as it was called at the time). The new fort, Fort St. Frederic, was completed in 1737, and held 120 soldiers. The fort consisted of a tower surrounded by masonry walls. Given its strategic position at the narrow point on the lake, as well as its twelve-foot-thick walls, Fort St. Frederic was a formidable fortification. Its tower was a four-story octagon with cannons on each floor. The limestone walls around it were almost eighteen feet high, with sentry boxes for keeping guard against the British.

A drawbridge provided entrance to the fort from the north, and visitors passed through a two-story guardhouse. On the first floor of the guardhouse were the guards' living quarters, and on the second floor were provisions for a hospital, as well as the living quarters for an interpreter for the local Indians. The main building of the fort was the redoubt. With twelve-foot-thick walls, it was strong enough to withstand British cannon fire. Within the building were twenty cannons, a powder magazine, living quarters for both officers and soldiers, a bakery, and an armory.

A windmill made of stone was built just south of the fort in 1740. Although it was intended as a gristmill for grinding grain, it also worked defensively, as it had several cannons mounted on its upper floor.

In order to maximize the French presence in the area, discourage British advancement, and encourage farming to help provision the fort, the French government awarded land to both civilians and soldiers, and encouraged them to settle in the area around the fort. They waived taxes for residents of the region as a further incentive. The population of French settled in the area soon numbered in the hundreds.

At the outbreak of the French and Indian War in 1754, the British decided to push back at the French. Plans were made to march on Fort St. Frederic. The French were aware of these plans, and hastily began building Fort Carillon to the south (later to be named Fort Ticonderoga). In 1758, General James Abercromby, leading an enormous contingent of British soldiers, advanced toward

Fort St. Frederic. He attacked Fort Carillon on the way, and was defeated. The British withdrew.

In 1759, the British had regrouped under General Jeffrey Amherst. The French troops, outnumbered approximately six to one, realized that they would be defeated. The civilians were evacuated, and the troops at Fort St. Frederic were reduced to approximately two hundred men. The civilian towns were razed so that they would not be able to be used by the British as they advanced.

Amherst laid siege to Carillon, and the French retreated. Before they left, they set fire to Fort Carillon, and then withdrew to Fort St. Frederic. As the British continued to advance, the French destroyed the redoubt and the stone windmill and then retreated. When Amherst reached Fort St. Frederic, he found much of the fort essentially intact. By August 4, the British were in possession of the fort. Across the river, the British could see a single chimney from a French settler's home still standing, which gave Chimney Point its name.

Amherst added new structures to Fort St. Frederic, now renamed "His Majesty's Fort of Crown Point." Ultimately, he enclosed seven acres within the fort, built timber and earthenworks that were over twenty-five feet tall, brought in a hundred cannons, and housed over four thousand soldiers in the fort.

In 1760, Colonel William Haviland led a force in an attack on Montreal, along with other British forces. Montreal, France's main stronghold, was defeated. The war continued, but the Champlain Valley was relatively peaceful. In 1763, the war ended with the signing of the Treaty of Paris. The British now controlled the previously French-held territories.

The next decade was relatively peaceful at Fort Crown Point. The British government was reluctant to invest much in the upkeep of the fort, so the site did deteriorate some during this period. As they retired, some soldiers were given land in the area, increasing the population of the region.

On April 21, 1773, a devastating fire broke out in the soldiers' barracks. Starting in the chimney, the fire spread to the wood shingles and walls of the fort. The soldiers were unable to put out the fire, which burned for more than three days, destroying the fort. The men remained, making their barracks in other outbuildings, and worked hard to recover any cannons or other usable items that survived the fire. The British were distressed at the destruction of the fort, but were reluctant to abandon the area. Instead, construction of an enlargement of Crown Point was planned.

Just as the British soldiers were getting underway to travel to Crown Point to enlarge it, Benedict Arnold and Ethan Allen captured Fort Ticonderoga, and then Crown Point. The colonial soldiers plundered the forts, sending more than sixty usable cannons and tons of ammunition to General Henry Knox, who transported it to Boston through a brutal winter.

By 1776, smallpox was taking its toll on the fort. By June, dozens were perishing from the disease every day. In July, the decision was made to move the army from Crown Point to Mount Independence, across the lake from Fort Ticonderoga. The sick were transported to Fort George. George Washington sent Colonel Thomas Hartley and his 6th Pennsylvania Battalion to man Crown Point. In August, the new American naval fleet met at Crown Point to be rigged for battle. They then proceeded northward, led by Benedict Arnold.

A naval battle occurred in October, off Valcour Island, some forty miles north of Crown Point. The Americans were defeated, burned their own boats, and retreated to Crown Point. Hartley then withdrew all troops from Crown Point. The British found the fort abandoned when they arrived on October 14, 1776. The British reinhabited the fort and held it for several more years, but turned it over to the Americans after the war.

The Town Today

The fort is currently ruins. The grounds at Fort Crown Point are open year-round, Monday through Friday from 8 A.M. to 3 P.M.. There is an onsite museum, which charges an admission fee and is open from May 15 to October 31. The museum is closed on Tuesdays and Wednesdays.

Directions

From Lake George, take Route 9 North/Lake Shore Drive. You will pass Fort Ticonderoga. Take a right onto Route 185 East/Bridge Road. Turn left into Adirondack Park Preserve.

REYNOLDSTON

A raucous dance hall once provided the entertainment for this lovely lumber town.

History

Little remains today of the busy community that once existed as Reynoldston. Reynoldston began life as a town called Brandon (founded in 1828), which grew from the nearby town of Bangor. Its first industry was making potash, or blacksalt. Potash is a type of fertilizer made from wood ashes and contains a significant amount of potassium, making it a sought-after commodity among farmers around Brandon.

Hiram Eddy, a local man, was one of the first in the area to earn a living through making potash. Eddy Road, one of the major thoroughfares in the town, was named for the trail that he carved through the woods, cutting trees to make into blacksalt. By the early 1870s, there were a few small sawmills functioning in the area, including the Webster Mill.

The Bordeaux family (Allen and Julia) was one of the earliest families in the area, followed in short order by Joseph Campbell and Orson Reynolds. Reynolds quickly purchased a great deal of land in the area, including the Webster Mill. He eventually accrued over ten thousand acres. He built a logging operation and sawmill, which attracted workers and their families. The town became informally known as Reynolds Mill, instead of Brandon. The name was officially changed to Reynoldston in 1894, when a U.S. post office was opened at the mill store.

The Reynolds's operations provided a livelihood and employment for many families in the area. At times, four separate logging camps were in action, cutting hard- and softwoods. As their prosperity grew, the Reynolds family increased their holdings to include other businesses. They developed a telephone and telegraph line, as well as a busy company store and various other holdings.

Like other lumber towns, the Reynolds Mill issued its own currency for a time. This "money," known as shinplasters, was only useful at the Reynolds Mill Store. This setup made the workers feel somewhat "owned" by the company, a common complaint among mill workers throughout the northeast.

As the town grew, the need for a school for the town's children became apparent. A one-room schoolhouse was built in 1880 (and would go on to outlast the mill and its operations by a decade and a half). Although the school had, at times, as many as sixty students for one teacher, many students dropped out before high school. Most sought work in the woods or the mill. Many local families could not afford to send their children to be boarded in Malone or Brushton in order to attend the high schools there.

Although the mill provided financial stability for the families in the area, other enterprises sprang up in Reynoldston as well. Farming, especially hops farming and maple sugaring, provided additional income for some Reynoldston families.

Housing in Reynoldston were not particularly varied. The lumber workers mostly lived in simple, gabled houses along the Eddy Road. The houses were usually built and owned by the Reynolds brothers and rented to the laborers. The homes typically had three rooms on the main level and two bedrooms on the upper floor. They were simply made, lacking stylish touches and decorations. The most elaborate house in Reynoldston was that of Newton Reynolds. Built around 1900, it was a Queen Anne–style home, with a viewing tower and a trophy room for Reynolds's many hunting trophies.

The community was fairly isolated. Far from any large towns, the families had to depend on one another for help and entertainment, especially during the brutally cold winters. One way some of the rowdier citizens occupied themselves was by visiting the Bordeaux Dance Hall, a large two-story square structure with a front porch. Ted and Miner Bordeaux opened the dance hall and bar in 1906, and it was successful until the town itself began to die out. It closed in 1919.

Besides the dance hall and bar, the enterprising Bordeaux brothers also included a barbershop, a store, and billiards. The lumberjacks in the area enjoyed the social opportunities, and on any given day, the front porch might have over a dozen men crowded together, enjoying libations and fun.

Dancing was held on the second floor of the building most Saturday nights. The dances attracted a wide range of people: young and old, poor and rich. Admission to the dance hall was free, unless you chose to dance. If you wished to dance, the cost was ten cents for the entire evening. Besides dancing, evening fun tended to be punctuated by brawls, especially among the men who had been drinking. The frequent fights kept Alley Bedor, the constable, very busy on weekends.

Other social activities were available to Reynoldston citizens. Dances were often held in peoples' kitchens, when four to eight friends would dance the Virginia Reel, waltzes, or square dances. Card parties were also common.

Religion was important in Reynoldston. Never large enough to warrant building its own church, the mostly Catholic population was serviced by traveling priests, who visited monthly. In addition, Allen Bordeaux and Philip Moquin also held Masses in their homes and included their neighbors. Mr. Bordeaux had apparently had some training as a priest. There were Protestants in the town as well. They held occasional services or revivals in the schoolhouse. Some of the families traveled to nearby towns such as Bangor for church services.

Holidays were special times in Reynoldston. The Reynolds's employees had Christmas off. Although few families had much money for gifts, they served a larger meal than ordinary, celebrated family, and enjoyed socializing and drinking. Families made home-made decorations and modest gifts. The Bordeaux family made small doughnuts and loaded a box of them onto a sled. They delivered the treats to the more impoverished children of the village. The local children put on Christmas musicals at the school, building the stage from lumber donated by the Reynolds family.

Many of the families in Reynoldston were French Canadian. Celebrating New Year's Eve by going from house to house, drinking and singing, was a tradition among many of the northern communities, and Reynoldston was no different. Beginning shortly after dark, the townsmen, rich and poor, shared drink and toasted the coming year.

In 1908, the Reynolds brothers signed a contract with the Brooklyn Cooperage to provide wooden staves for their barrels. The contract ran for a decade, at the end of which the hardwood forests on the 10,000-acre tract that the Reynoldses owned had been decimated. Following the depletion of the hardwoods, the softwoods were cut and shipped to the Malone Paper Company, until few trees remained.

By 1921, it was clear that the wood industry in Reynoldston was finished. The company's assets were liquidated, the company store was shut down, and the townspeople began to witness the end of the town as they knew it. The mill was closed in 1925. Families began leaving the area in search of work. The Reynolds family sold off most of the land to the state of New York. The school closed in the 1940s. By the 1970s only a few elderly citizens remained in Reynoldston.

The Town Today

Little remains of the original Reynoldston. Some of the houses along the Eddy Road are the original workers' homes.

Directions

From the Watertown area, take Route 11 north to Potsdam. In Potsdam, take Route 11B toward the east. Turn right onto County Route 15/Eddy Road. The Reynoldston site is .4 miles past Quarry Road.

FORT WILLIAM HENRY

The fort immortalized in James Fenimore Cooper's *Last of the Mohicans* continues to shock visitors with its bloody, tragic history.

History

The French and Indian War, also known as the Seven Years' War, was fought between British and French troops, along with their Native American allies. It spanned the years between 1754 and 1761 and symbolized the struggle between the European superpowers to claim the new American frontier. While the British ultimately won, the many battles and skirmishes were brutal and deadly, and remain an important part of the history of the U.S. and Canada.

Fort William Henry, on Lake George, was in service starting on November 13, 1755, under William Eyre. The forward-thinking Eyre had altered the traditional British fort design. Typically, British forts were rather simple, consisting of walls of vertical logs surrounded by a moat, or by an earthen dyke. Eyre instead constructed Fort William Henry with some French innovations: sand-filled walls that were thirty feet thick, and diamond-shaped corner bastions.

The interior of the fort consisted of four barracks buildings of log construction surrounding a central parade ground. Two of the barracks were two stories high, with exterior stairs. The other two barracks had basements. A hospital was located at the southeast end of the parade ground, and the powder magazine was located beneath the northeast corner bastion. A moat encircled the fort on three sides. The moat contained a line of stockade posts and a bridge to enter the fort. The soldiers' vegetable gardens were in the northern and western areas of the fort. A privy jutted out over Lake George at the northeast corner of the fort.

The fort's inhabitants lived a rather wretched life. Poor sanitary conditions and illnesses such as smallpox took a significant toll on the inhabitants. Visitors to the fort noted that five to eight deaths per day was not unusual. The horrific smell of the fort was remarked upon in letters from visiting commanders. Most of the pestilence was blamed on the American (also known as Provincial) troops, who tended to be looked upon with disdain by their British counterparts.

In 1757 Lieutenant Colonel George Munro had taken over as commander of the fort. That summer, rumors circulated that Fort William Henry was to be attacked by the French. In response, Munro was sent additional troops: the 60th Royal American Regiment, the Massachusetts Provincials, and the New York Provincials. These new soldiers brought the population of the fort to 2,372 men—not including the significant number of ill men or the family members and camp followers associated with the fort.

In August, the rumors of imminent attack came true. Led by the formidable Marquis de Montcalm, a force of over 8,000 (reports vary about the exact size of the attacking force) French and Indians from Fort Carillon approached Fort William Henry.

The French and Indian forces attacked from across Lake George, traveling in boats, while others marched by land from the west. The French had brought their cannons, which they floated on rafts. The Canadians quickly dug trenches each night as they surrounded the fort, preparing to lay siege. The shelling of Fort William Henry began on August 3, 1757.

Jabez Fitch Jr., a soldier from nearby Fort Edward, kept an account of the battle from his perspective:

> August 3: I Hered ye Morning Gun Fire at ye Lake Before ours—a little after Sun Rise we Here he Cannon Fire Briskly at ye Lake and also ye Small arms we Immediately Contluded that they were Attacted—This Firing Lasted Most of ye Day.

> August 4: I Hear By ye Prisoner that Colyar Brought in that the French Have Got a Vary Strong army against Fort Wm Henry He Said there was 6000 Ragulars & 5000 Canadians.

> August 5: Before Sunrise We Heard Ye Canon Play Vary Brisk at ye Lake Soon after ye Small arms Began to Fire

this Firing Lated all Day without Much Ceasing it was Contluded that this Day there was ye Most Ammunition Expended that Ever was in a Day at that Plais Before.

August 9: We Had a Rumer about Noon that Fort Wm Henry was Taken for their Firing Seasd Some time in ye Morning.

After six days of shelling, Munro surrendered the fort. A factor in the loss was the failure of the British cannons and mortars, many of which exploded behind the fort walls due to metal fatigue. On August 9, the British commanders realized that no more help would be coming from Fort Edward, and that surrender was the only reasonable option.

The terms of the surrender stated that the British and provincial troops were allowed to take their personal belongings and march to Fort Edward, with the promise that they would not fight against the French for eighteen months. The sick and wounded were to be left in Fort William Henry to be tended to until they were well enough to vacate the fort. Montcalm explained the terms of the surrender to his Native American allies.

The Indians with Montcalm's contingent were outraged. They had been promised the ability to scalp the British and provincial troops. Scalps were prized trophies of battles, and raised the status of Indian men who hung them outside their homes. Men with many scalps tended to be viewed as very brave, and were viewed as desirable husbands by Indian women. The French decision to be generous to the soldiers from Fort William Henry was unthinkable to the Indian allies.

As soon as the British and provincials had left the fort to march to Fort Edward, several of the Indians with Montcalm raced into Fort William Henry and attacked the ill and injured within. They killed and scalped seventeen weakened soldiers, along with several women and children.

Other Indians joined the first group and plundered the fort's cemetery, digging up the bodies buried there. Their intent was to steal red coats and blankets, as well as the scalps of the cadavers. Unfortunately for the grave robbers, many of the dead had died of smallpox, which had infected the items they were buried with.

The next day, on August 10, Abenaki Indians attacked the rear of the retreating line of unarmed refugees from Fort William Henry. Soldiers from New Hampshire and their families, who made up much of the end of the marching line, suffered the greatest losses.

It is unclear whether or not the French soldiers escorting the line did anything to quell the bloodbath. The attacking Indians murdered and scalped between two hundred and twelve hundred people (depending on the historical source), and hundreds were kidnapped to be marched north to Canada for ransom.

Colonel Munro and his senior officers escaped the murderous frenzy and were taken to the French camp. Munro was later escorted with the remaining five hundred or so surviving soldiers to Fort Edward. Fort William Henry was dismantled.

Jabez Fitch Jr. journaled:

> Ye Indians Beset our People & Kild them with their Speers Robd them of all that they were allowed by ye Capitulation. Children they took from their Mothers and Dasht their Brains out against ye Stons ye Mothers they Served ye Same and also their Husbands if they offerd to Relieve them So.

Colonel Frye, who barely escaped the carnage, described the massacre:

> [The Indians] began to take the Officers Hatts, Swords, Guns, & Cloaths, Striping them all to their Shirts, and on some officers Left no Shirt at all. While this was doing they Killd & Scalpt all the Sick & wounded before our faces, then took out from Our troops, all the Indians and negroes and Carried them off. One of the former they burnt alive afterwards.

When the Indians attacked the rear of the column, Colonel Frye described it as follows:

> Officers, privates, Women & Children, Some of which Latter they killed & Scalp'd in the Road. This horrid Scene of Blood & Slaughter Obliged our Officers to apply to the Officers of the French guard for protection, which they refused, and told them, they must take to the Woods, and Shift for themselves, which many did.

Montcalm later intervened with the marauding Indians, securing the release of approximately four hundred kidnapped people. Approximately two hundred more remained in Canada to be ransomed or sold into slavery.

The British people were outraged when news of the massacre spread. Montcalm, who had promised to protect the surrendering troops, suffered great damage to his impressive reputation. Prior to the siege, Montcalm's assistant journaled that he feared that the Indian chiefs would not be able to restrain the younger braves. Afterward, he expressed fear that Europe might believe that the Indians did not act alone, and that the French were complicit. In reality, the French surely had little control over their Native American allies, and were likely horrified at what they witnessed. The British government decided not to rebuild Fort William Henry, although British troops did camp on the site several times as they sought revenge on the French garrisons in the area.

In 1854, the grand Fort William Henry Hotel opened just north of where the fort had stood. The successful resort burned down in 1908, but was quickly rebuilt, reopening in 1911.

In 1952, excavation on the actual fort site began, with the intent of reconstructing the fort as a tourist attraction. British fort plans, coupled with the tireless work of archaeologist Stanley Gifford and his team, helped to provide a remarkably accurate vision of the former fort. A full-sized, historically accurate version of the fort was built. Throughout the excavation period, evidence from the massacre was evident in the form of skulls with scalp marks and skeletons with other signs of trauma.

James Fenimore Cooper's *The Last of the Mohicans* contains a fictionalized and rather inaccurate version of the siege and resulting massacre at Fort William Henry. But while his characters and much of his storyline were fiction, the massacre at Fort William Henry was very real, and left an indelible stain in the history of the French and Indian War.

The Town Today

The fort is open daily to visitors from May through October, from 9 A.M. to 6 P.M. The fort is built to be a very accurate representation of the original fort. There is an admission charge for entry. Guided tours and ghost tours are available.

Directions

Fort William Henry is located on Route 9 just south of Lake George Village. From Interstate 87, take Exit 21 to the village. The fort is located on the north (right) side of the road. Parking is available near the fort.

CAMP SANTANONI

One of over thirty "great camps" in the Catskills, Camp Santanoni was widely regarded as the grandest of the Adirondack camps.

History

Camp Santanoni was created by a wealthy Albany banker and businessman, Robert C. Pruyn. Mr. Pruyn and his family enjoyed using the camp as a way to escape the stress of city life, as well as a place to entertain business clients. Visitors to the camp included Theodore Roosevelt and James Fenimore Cooper.

Camp Santanoni was 12,900 acres, and was made up of three separate groupings of buildings: The Gate Lodge Complex, the Great

Camp Complex, and the Farm Complex. A friend of Mr. Pruyn, Robert H. Robertson, designed the majority of the camp. The two men had become friends at Yale. Robertson had gained some fame for designing many early skyscrapers in New York City.

There is a Japanese influence to some of the architecture in the camp. The most apparent Japanese-inspired design is the single roof and porch that connects several buildings. The dominant roof of the complex is "stepped" and when seen from above resembles the "bird in flight" that one often notes in Japanese architecture. Pruyn's father, Robert H. Pruyn, had served as minister to Japan under President Abraham Lincoln, and the camp owner had served as secretary to his father. Clearly, Pruyn valued the beautiful lines of Japanese architecture and incorporated them into his much-loved retreat.

The Gate Lodge Complex is located near Newcomb, NY. It includes a large lodge building containing six staff bedrooms. It also boasts an impressive gateway arch, a caretaker's house, and several barns and other outbuildings.

The Farm Complex is approximately a mile farther into the camp. The farm supplied the camp with meat and produce; extra products, especially dairy, were sold in Newcomb or sent to the Pruyns in Albany. Bottles embossed with "Santanoni" are treasured in the Newcomb area. The Farm Complex is composed of huge barns, three farmhouses, and staff cottages. There is also a stone creamery in which butter and cheese was made, a workshop, a chicken coop, kennels, a smokehouse, and other structures.

The Great Lodge Complex is approximately 4.7 miles from the Gate Complex. It is situated on the edge of Newcomb Lake and boasts a gorgeous view of the Adirondack Mountains. The main lodge actually comprised six separate buildings, all with a Japanese flavor to their architecture. One building contained the main living and dining area and had two bedrooms upstairs. Four other cabins contained a total of seven bedrooms; they were connected by a common roof and porch to another building containing a large kitchen and seven staff bedrooms. The architecture and building materials are considered to be some of the finest examples of Adirondack architecture. The buildings were made of spruce, and the walls were covered with birch bark. Hand-hewn beams and soaring ceilings greeted visitors, who were charmed by the massive fieldstone fireplaces.

After enjoying the property for decades, the Pruyn family sold it in 1953 to the Melvin family of Syracuse. The Melvins enjoyed the camp for almost two more decades, although they did not maintain the grandeur of the property to the degree that the Pruyns had.

Then, in 1971, an unspeakable tragedy struck. Douglas Legg, the Melvins' eight-year-old grandson, disappeared in the forest at Santanoni. No trace of him was ever found. The Melvin family, devastated by the loss, left the property, wishing never to return. They sold the property to the Adirondack Conservancy Committee (part of the Nature Conservancy).

The State of New York purchased the complex from the conservancy in 1972. The state allowed the property to fall into disrepair, with the intent of removing the improvements to the property and allowing it to retain a "forever wild" state. With urging from the nearby Town of Newcomb, as well as several preservation groups, the state decided to make efforts to preserve the remaining structures on the site. The camp was classified as a National Historical Landmark in 2000 and is now open to the public.

The Town Today

Camp Santanoni is a lovely retreat for the public. The camp is open all year long; however, many of the building interiors are open seasonally (July 1 through Labor Day), so if you are planning on visiting, plan accordingly. Interpretive staff are on hand.

The property is handicapped-accessible. For example, on the 4.7-mile road to the Great Lodge Complex, which does not allow motorized vehicles, mobility-impacted visitors may call ahead to have an accessible horse and wagon transport them. The covered porch is accessible by ramp, and accessible horse-mounting platforms are available.

A fire destroyed the dairy and horse barns in 2004, but the ruins can be viewed. Other ruins of structures that deteriorated and fell into great disrepair are also present. The 15,000-square-foot main lodge, a stone artist's studio, a boathouse, and many other small structures survive. Fewer than half of the original structures remain.

Directions

From the NYS Thruway (I-90), take Exit 27 at Amsterdam. Take Route 30 through several small villages, such as Speculator, Indian Lake, and Blue Mountain Lake. In Long Lake, turn onto Route 28 N to Newcomb. Camp Santanoni is located on Route 28 N between Newcomb's Town Hall and Aunt Polly's Bed and Breakfast.

FORT EDWARD/ROGERS ISLAND

The U.S. Army Rangers' long history began at Rogers Island. The tactics used by the men there revolutionized warfare.

History

The initial structure on the site of Fort Edward was a fairly primitive stockade named Fort Nicholson. Fort Nicholson, named for Colonel Francis Nicholson, was built in approximately 1709, during Queen Anne's War, part of the struggle between France and England for command of the New World. Fort Nicholson was manned by approximately 450 British soldiers and comprised a stockade, the log structures that housed the soldiers, and various storehouses.

In 1731, at the end of Queen Anne's War, the fort was transformed into a trading post under a Dutch trader named John Henry Lydius. Lydius, claiming ownership of the land because of a deed dated from 1696, traded from the land for many years. The area became known as Fort Lydius.

Records disagree about the next few years. Some sources say that Lydius's home and businesses were destroyed in 1745, as French and

Indian raids increased along the Hudson River. At some point around the middle of the century, the land became the property of England.

In August 1755, the British began construction of Fort Edward either adjacent to or on the site of the former trading post, in response to the beginning of the French and Indian War. General William Johnson chose Captain William Eyre to design the fort; Eyre also designed Fort William Henry at Lake George (see page 85). These two forts became the forerunners of the British efforts to command the colonies. The new fort was initially named Fort Lyman, after Major General Phineas Lyman, Johnson's second-in-command. Within a month, however, Johnson had changed his mind, and named it Fort Edward, after the Duke of York, Edward Augustus.

Eyre designed the new fort to be even larger than Fort William Henry. It was situated on the bank of the Hudson River and was surrounded by a moat and earthworks. Within the fort, there were extensive barracks, a hospital, a guardhouse, a blacksmith shop, and a powder magazine. The British soldiers lived in the barracks within the fort and also within the defensive lines north and east of the fort, along what is present-day Route 4.

The fort itself was part of a much-larger system of structures, including Rogers Island, across an inlet in the Hudson River, and eight blockhouses in the area. Many tents were erected on Rogers Island to house the impressive number of troops housed there. A bridge was built for access from Fort Edward to Rogers Island.

In 1757, a large smallpox hospital was built on Rogers Island. There were also large gardens for vegetables, "necessary houses" (outhouses), and a sawpit. To provide for the needs of the soldiers, merchants opened shops in the area; a brewery also was opened nearby and began producing spruce beer in 1759.

During the summers, the numbers of British and provincial troops in the fort and surrounding areas reached as many as sixteen thousand, making Fort Edward one of the largest "cities" in the New World. As cold weather settled in each year, the main body of the garrison left the wilds to return to the comfort of Albany for the winter. They left behind a small garrison to pass the bitterly cold months at the fort until spring returned.

One of the most significant contributions of Fort Edward was the birth of what later became the United States Army Rangers. From 1756 to 1759, Captain Robert Rogers and his contingent, dubbed "Rogers' Rangers," camped in small log buildings on Rogers Island. On March 23, 1756, Rogers started the rangers with sixty privates, three sergeants, one lieutenant, and one ensign. In time, Rogers' Rangers grew to a force of four hundred men and had a well-deserved reputation as an effective, important battalion.

In 1757, Robert Rogers wrote his "Ranging Rules," which outlined the principles of forest warfare. He later wrote "Standing Rules" in 1759, which provided some of the framework for today's Army Rangers.

Some of the rules were as follows:

When you're on the march, act the way you would if you was sneaking up on a deer. See the enemy first.

When you're on the march we march single file, far enough apart so no one shot can't go through two men.

If we strike on soft ground, we spread out abreast, so it's hard to track us.

When we camp, half the party stays awake while the other half sleeps.

If somebody's trailing you, make a circle, come back onto your tracks, and ambush the folks that aim to ambush you.

Don't cross a river by a regular ford.

Some of the members of Rogers' group were Mohican Indians. Rogers listened closely to these men and learned from their form of warfare, which influenced his Ranging Rules and Standing Rules. They taught Rogers their style of forest warfare, which was very different from traditional British or French warfare.

British soldiers often wore bright red coats. Rogers, on the other hand, dressed his men in green jackets, brown leggings, moccasins, and a flat Scottish cap. While the British and French fought very traditionally, in lines, firing weapons in volleys, Rogers' men spread out, went low to the ground to fire, used the camouflage of the forest to their advantage, and used Mohican tracking strategies. Rogers' Rangers made many forays, including attacks on Ticonderoga and on Abnaki villages.

One of the most famous roles of Fort Edward was its actions—or rather, inaction—during the siege of Fort William Henry (see page 85). Criticism has been leveled at Fort Edward's commander, General Webb, for not providing help to Fort William Henry.

Fort Edward, or more accurately, Rogers Island, also provided the staging area for General Abercrombie's ill-fated attack on Fort Carillon (later Ticonderoga) in 1758. Following the battle, Abercrombie's injured men returned to Fort Edward to the hospitals there.

The death of Duncan Campbell on July 18, 1758, was a significant loss to the British. Major Campbell was of the Forty-Second Highland Regiment. He was mortally wounded at Ticonderoga on July 9, and carried to Fort Edward where he died nine days later. He was immortalized in Robert Louis Stevenson's story "Ticonderoga: A Legend of the West Highlands," published in *Scribner's Magazine* in 1887. In it, Campbell was at his family castle in Scotland, when he was visited by the ghost of his cousin, who had been murdered. His cousin said, "Farewell, till we meet at Ticonderoga," before disappearing.

Following Abercrombie's defeat, Fort Edward again acted as a staging area, this time for General Amherst as he prepared to march on Fort Ticonderoga. This time, the British were successful. The British then established their stronghold at Ticonderoga and Crown Point, rendering Fort Edward much less critical. It became a base for supplying the more important forts, and troop numbers dwindled. The fort was abandoned in 1780. The modern town of Fort Edward grew up around the remains of the old fort.

The Town Today

Rogers Island is open from 10 A.M. to 4 P.M. Tuesday through Saturday from mid-May through October 31. Admission is free (although donations are welcome), and it is handicapped-accessible. There are restrooms and a gift shop, and picnic sites are available.

Rogers Island hosts archaeology students, and impressive digs have taken place on the island. It is viewed as one of the more "pristine" sites still existing from the French and Indian War and is worth a visit.

Fort Edward itself did not fare as well. Along present-day Route 4, one can find many markers indicating the sites of earthworks, moats, and so on. Many homes in the town of Fort Edward have beams and rocks in their cellars from the original fort. However, few structures from the original fort are still visible.

Directions

To reach Rogers Island from I-87, take Exit 17N onto Route 9 North. Turn right at the second traffic light onto Route 197 East. Turn right on Rogers Island after crossing first bridge.

To reach Rogers Island from Route 4: In the village of Fort Edward, take Route 197 West. Turn left on Rogers Island just before the second bridge.

Western New York

ONEIDA COMMUNITY

Ironically, the company that manufactures the silverware that so many brides register for was originated by a polyamorous society.

History

Founded in 1848, Oneida Community was an effective, successful commune for over thirty years. Started by John Humphrey Noyes, Oneida Community was intended as a gathering of the faithful in preparation for the impending return of Christ.

A fierce socialist, Noyes took pride in leading one of the most successful and long-lasting of the many Utopian communities in existence in the 1800s. As a young man, Noyes came to believe that he was different from other men, divinely superior to them. He believed that God had chosen him to provide a foundation of God's kingdom on earth.

Although raised in a devout home, Noyes turned away from his religion in his teenage years, choosing instead to indulge "the lust of the eye and the pride of life," as he later said. His interest in women became a focus in his life, and proved to be an effective distraction from his family's spiritual path.

In September 1831, while vacationing in Vermont, Noyes attended a religious revival in Putney, at his mother's request. Listening to the religious rhetoric and seeing the devotion of the followers, Noyes experienced a religious crisis, questioning his current earthly path. At that point he dedicated himself utterly to the pursuit of service to God. He believed in Perfectionism, the belief that one could completely be freed from sin.

Noyes initially set up a commune at Putney. The believers there not only had to live by Noyes's religious views, but were also required to formally vow obedience to him and his spiritual authority.

Years later, Noyes required much the same level of subservience from his followers at Oneida Community. Although he no longer required a written obedience contract, he still demanded that all members acknowledge his authority and superiority. Rebellious members were dealt with sternly, and faced possible expulsion if their disobedience persisted. Noyes viewed such rumblings from his followers as rebellion against God himself. When asked why he was not subject to the same criticism as his followers, Noyes replied that he was spiritually superior to other men. No one less prominent than Christ, St. Paul, or John the Baptist returning to earth would be fit for the task of criticizing him.

Early in the Putnam group's existence, Noyes's views on marriage and male-female relations were much in line with those of the rest of society. He frowned upon the way single men and women flirted and stole some private moments at Perfectionist gatherings. He worried that it tarnished the morally pure stance of the group.

Then, in the winter of 1835, Noyes and a male follower were visiting Brimfield, New York. While there, they met some attractive female followers. As they parted after a religious discussion, one of the women boldly kissed Noyes. He was taken by surprise, and conflicted about the emotions that the woman's boldness awakened in him. Noyes began to fear the strength of these new emotions.

While Noyes was mulling over his amorous feelings, his traveling companion, Simon Lovett, was not so successful in defeating his demons. One of the other attractive women had sneaked into his room, and did not leave until morning. Both denied any wrongdoing, but the "Brimfield Bundling" incident provided fodder for detractors of Perfectionism.

Back in Vermont, Noyes's father, having heard the gossip, was appalled at what had taken place in Brimfield. He demanded that Noyes distance himself from Lovett. Instead, Noyes drew closer to his friend, inviting him to preach with him at various religious meetings. Noyes's father, enraged, cut his son off financially, and angrily confronted him. Noyes angrily left Putney, and lived as a homeless person for several years throughout New England, traveling by foot, bathing infrequently, and often thought by locals to be insane. He ranted and raved to anyone who would listen about Perfectionism.

After several years of this meager existence, Noyes decided to split from Perfectionism, instead deciding to surround himself with a few devoted followers. After recruiting several family members, Noyes found that having just a few followers was not enough for him. He moved to Ithaca, New York, to start a newspaper in which he could teach others his views.

Around this time he began pursuing a woman named Abigail Merwin, with whom he believed he had an unbreakable bond forged by God Himself. He proposed marriage to her, but she was not moved by his devotion. Although he sent her letters promising to wait for years for her to decide to marry him, he quickly turned his attentions to a thirty-year-old woman named Harriet Holton.

Harriet was due to inherit a significant estate from her father, who was a former U.S. senator from Vermont. There were apparently no romantic feelings between Noyes and Harriet. Noyes often described his marriage to Harriet as a partnership, not a loving marriage. Indeed, before their marriage, sensing his lack of ardor, Harriet suggested that they live together as a form of siblings. Noyes, however, adamantly demanded a true marriage, as he wanted to leave his celibacy in the past. They married on June 28, 1838.

Slowly, Noyes began to gather followers. One such member was Mary Cragin. A married former schoolteacher who appears rather dour in photos, she had a well-earned reputation for being amorous, and she and Noyes carried on a torrid relationship for many years. His views of his own superiority and his changing views on sexuality drove some followers away, but those who remained tended to be very loyal.

Noyes was a fervent believer in science, despite his spiritual devotion. Although he believed in miracles and occasionally attempted to cure his followers by laying on his hands, he also had a ravenous interest in science. Noyes was a proponent of eugenics, the belief that the human race could become superior through selective breeding, a concept that he refered to as "stirpiculture." The Oneidans began their stirpiculture initiative in 1869, with parents being chosen based on their level of spiritual devoutness. Over fifteen percent of the stirpicult children born at Oneida were fathered by Noyes, further proof of his own belief in his superior spiritual standing.

In 1846, Noyes's views on sexual relations had changed considerably from his initial rigid stance that spiritual leaders should not even hug or kiss their followers. He began to believe that Christians in an advanced state of holiness could engage in polyamorous activities. He believed that marriage, in the traditional sense, was not God's plan, but that "free love" would please God more. During this time, Noyes had fallen deeply in love with Mary Cragin, who has been described as "irresistible to men." Other men in the community, including Noyes's own brother-in-law, fell in love with her as well. Although Noyes's wife, Harriet, accepted Noyes's views on free love, she did struggle with jealousy toward Mary Cragin.

Noyes felt that the "complex marriage" that his group would engage in should have structure and some rules. For example, prior to consummating the relationship, the interested potential lovers were encouraged to enter into discussions with all involved parties, including spouses.

Acknowledging the controversial nature of the practice, the group kept their complex marriage practice a closely guarded secret for some time. However, in 1847 Noyes was arrested for adultery. As public opinion raged, and the threat of mob action against the group roiled, Noyes fled, finding a new home for the Perfectionists: Oneida, New York.

Noyes was invited to the area by a fellow Perfectionist who had bought land and a sawmill on the Oneida Indian Reservation. Soon the Putney Perfectionists followed Noyes and settled in. The community began to grow into a robust group. By the beginning of 1849, the group included eighty-seven members.

Noyes believed that the community should all live within the same house and be a family, instead of an "Association," as it was called at the time. The group purchased an 80-acre farm on which they built the Mansion House. The house was impressive and elegant. It was three stories high and included a dormitory for unmarried men and boys. The third floor of the mansion had a large sleeping area for women and married people. In the interest of privacy, "tents" were created in this area, consisting of curtains that could be drawn when needed.

The early years of the Oneida Community were financially lean, as the group strove to support itself while remaining tight-knit. Initially, they attempted to grow fruit and vegetables, but found that it was difficult to make enough money to support the community. Later they manufactured and sold animal traps. The trap business was lucrative, and included customers such as the Hudson Bay Company. By the late 1850s, the Oneida Community's sales were exceeding 100,000 traps per year. By 1865, they were selling 275,000 per year.

The Oneidans were an inventive, industrious group of people. They invented several items that are still in use today. They invented a rudimentary washing machine, the lazy Susan, a mechanical mop-wringer, a mechanical potato peeler, and a garter belt that did not cut off circulation to the legs while holding up one's stockings. In 1877, they began manufacturing silverware, which continues to be sold today.

At night, the Oneidans met in the family hall of the mansion. At these meetings, which were rather informal, the members read the news, sewed, and discussed God, house repairs, and child-rearing. Essentially, it was the time for the members to catch up with one another and take care of community business.

One of the key beliefs of the community was that criticism was beneficial to the soul. A member would sit quietly while the other members (or sometimes a "criticism commission") sat around them, listing their every fault.

The Oneidans were a relatively healthy, long-lived group of individuals. The community believed that their godliness was the reason for the good health of the members. In truth, their semi-isolation, excellent diet, exercise, and fresh air are likely the reason that most illnesses that swept through the nation were not seen at Oneida. The Oneidans, however, believed that sickness occurred when the body was invaded by an evil spirit.

An example of this belief occurred when several members of the community died of diphtheria. Noyes blamed a member named William Mills of "malignant sorcery" in weakening the spiritual citadel of Oneida. Mills had been recently convicted of making inappropriate sexual advances toward two preteen girls in the local community, which gave Oneida a black eye in the eyes of the public.

The Oneidans were not all as sure as Noyes that God alone was protecting them from disease. At times, they brought in doctors and secular treatments, which Noyes vehemently opposed. Noyes believed that, in addition to faith, a sick member would benefit from a healthy dose of criticism from the others. When someone fell ill, a criticism committee would convene to publicly catalog all the shortcomings of the ill person. Many members credited their criticism sessions as key components in their recoveries from illnesses.

Childrearing at Oneida was conducted differently from in the outside world. The Oneidans believed that the strong bonds between parents and children (like those between traditional spouses) were unhealthy and promoted neuroses and the sins of jealousy and worshiping graven images. Noyes believed that children belonged to God and the community, and not to their biological parents.

If a couple wanted to bear a child, they first brought their request to the community. If approved, they sought pregnancy. For the first year after delivering the baby, the mothers were allowed to focus on the baby and were relieved of their usual chores. At the end of that year, the child was turned over to the Children's House, where he or she was raised by appointed caregivers. Children were told who their parents were, except in cases of accidental pregnancies in which the father was unknown. However, parents who persisted in trying to parent their children beyond the first year were often punished by being forbidden to have contact with the child for a length of time.

The Oneida children were discouraged from playing with dolls. Mary Cragin, Noyes's favorite mistress and the first headmistress of Oneida, believed that they encouraged the children to playact unhealthy parental attachment. Dolls were compared to idols and graven images. All of the young girls were made to throw their toy dolls into a fire.

While he was at Oneida, Noyes's initial arrest was finally addressed. Noyes agreed to put an end to the complex marriage practices, and the charges against him were dropped. However, within a few months, when the eyes of the law had moved on, Noyes reinstated the practices at Oneida.

In part because of the interest in its polyamourous practices, Oneida became a successful tourist attraction. Famous entertainers and lecturers visited (including the Norwegian violinist Ole Bull, whose own ghost town, New Norway, is covered in *Pennsylvania Ghost Towns*). On most summer Sundays, tourists flocked to the community. They strolled the lovely grounds, listened to the community's band, and purchased refreshments.

Sex at Oneida followed rules and was not the free-for-all that was seen at some polyamorous societies of the time. For instance, when young men came of age, they were paired with older women, including postmenopausal women. The women would instruct and "train" the men in the practices of complex marriage. Young women entering adulthood were trained almost exclusively by Noyes, which later became a source of contention in the group.

Traditional relationship taboos were sometimes not observed at Oneida. For example, Noyes reportedly carried on an affair with his niece, Tirzah, and stated publicly that he wished to have a child with her. She did have a child with Noyes's brother, George, while Noyes had a child with another niece, Helen Miller.

Noyes's son with Mary Cragin, Victor, did not share his father's religious views. Unable to accept this perceived rebellion, Noyes had Victor declared insane and committed to a Utica asylum. He was later returned to Oneida and granted breeding privileges by his father. Mary Cragin died in July 1851, when her boat capsized in the Hudson River, drowning her. She was mourned by the community, where she was much loved.

Noyes realized that his reign at Oneida would not last forever. He began to groom his son Theodore to succeed him. Theodore was not universally loved as Noyes was. He was described as bossy and haughty in his dealings with others. Noyes began placing increasing responsibility on Theodore to take over the business management of the community. Members of the community protested against Theodore's secretive approach to managing the businesses, and Theodore and Noyes found themselves under siege. In 1872, Theodore had a nervous breakdown and left Oneida for several months. Upon his return to the community, he confessed that he had strong doubts about the existence of God.

Noyes was horrified that his heir apparent was suddenly unacceptable to the community in the most fundamental way. He strove to find another role for his beloved son. Noyes had become interested in communing with spirits, such as those of Christ and the Apostles. Because of Theodore's agnosticism, Noyes felt that putting him in charge of proving the existence of the spirit world would keep him in the community and possibly lead him back to Christianity.

Theodore took to his new job with enthusiasm. He found several Oneidans who could serve as mediums. He traveled the area, seeking proof of the ability to communicate with ghosts. Theodore's secular views continued to be controversial and disturbing to many community members. In 1877, Noyes briefly stepped down to allow Theodore to lead, but this only increased the disquiet in the group. Theodore was unable to unify the group, and Noyes returned to power in 1878.

One of the more controversial decisions during Theodore's reign was that all sexual liaisons had to be reported in writing to Theodore. The intent was to ensure fairness in attention given to any particular member. But the rule instead caused resentment and perceived restriction on the community's sexual behavior.

Theodore had fallen in love with a woman who Noyes found threatening, Ann Bailey. Theodore appointed her as the women's superintendent. While in that position, she was accused of separating couples in order to secure the men's attention for herself. Noyes found himself intervening to prevent members from leaving the community to escape Ann's regime.

Noyes asked Ann to resign, and when she did not, he moved to remove her both from her job and from Theodore. Enraged, Theodore expressed his support of Ann by resigning from his own post. However, he remained at Oneida, while Ann did not. She moved on and later married Joseph Skinner, another former Oneida Community member. With Ann gone, Noyes abolished the system of reporting all sexual relationships in writing in an effort to reunify the community.

The community, however, was beginning to change. The impending Kingdom of God that the followers had been expecting had not materialized. Some Oneidans began to lose their faith. In addition, Noyes himself began to lose his grip on the community. As he aged, young women were less interested in having him take on the role of "first husband." This weakened his ability to influence not only the women, but also the men who the women later took as lovers.

Other men in the community began to question Noyes's role, including why he was the only one allowed to initiate the young women into complex marriage. Noyes felt besieged by the rumblings of discontent. Another threat to the community was the fact that the younger members of the community were finding complex marriage unsatisfying. Many members were seeking traditional, monogamous marriage.

The moral tenor of the public at large had become more strict in the years since Oneida was founded. Public perception of the practices at Oneida had become poisonous. In the summer of 1879, the New York courts had begun taking testimony about the practices at Oneida, comparing them publicly to Mormon polygamists. A Syracuse newspaper reported that Noyes was going to be arrested.

The night after the newspaper article came out, Noyes sneaked out of the mansion in his socks in the middle of the night and fled to Canada. He moved in with a Perfectionist family outside London, Ontario. He later moved to a large stone cottage in Niagara Falls, which had been provided by the Oneida Community.

With Noyes gone, the community began to change. Traditional marriages became sanctioned. Children were allowed to remain with their biological parents. Basic tenets of the Oneida Perfectionist community were ignored and dismissed.

Ultimately, the community became unrecognizable from Noyes's vision. The silverware factory, which had provided a considerable portion of the group's income, moved to the Niagara Falls area, as did many community members. Many others stayed on at the mansion, but they mingled more with the outside world. The remaining members tended to be embarrassed at the public's views on their former lifestyles, and sought to distance themselves from those practices. The community's children were frequently referred to as "bastards" by the local townspeople.

Noyes died in Niagara Falls on April 13, 1886, with Theodore by his side. He was interred in the Oneida Community's cemetery. His simple gravestone was the same as everyone else's, in line with his communistic beliefs.

The remaining Oneidans threw themselves into the tableware business. The new president of the Oneida Community Ltd., John

Lord, regularly consulted with Noyes through mediums from beyond the grave.

The Town Today

Some descendants of the original community continue to live in the area. The Mansion House still stands, and houses some of these descendants. It also houses the Oneida Corporation's visiting business people. Tours are available to visitors, and rooms are available for overnight lodging. In a final irony, traditional weddings are often performed on the lovely grounds.

Directions

From the west, via the New York State Thruway (Route 90), take the Verona exit, number 33, and turn left onto Route 365 West. Turn left onto Route 5 East. At the first light (West Hamilton Avenue in Sherrill, NY) turn right. Turn right at the next light onto Sherrill Road. After crossing Oneida Creek, Sherrill Road becomes Kenwood Avenue. Across from the administration building for Oneida Ltd., turn right onto Skinner Road. Park behind the building.

FORT NIAGARA

Fort Niagara's influence spanned centuries, not decades. It flew three nations' flags at various times, and served a vital strategic function in several wars.

History

In the early 1600s, France occupied Quebec as far as the St. Lawrence River, and would have liked to expand into the Niagara region. However, the Native Americans in the area, the Five Nations of the Iroquois, were unfriendly toward the French, and hindered their expansion through New York colony. The Five Nations included the Oneida, Mohawk, Onandaga, Cayuga, and Seneca tribes. Archaeological evidence suggests that the site of the future Fort Niagara was used intermittently by the Indians as a fishing and hunting camp during the mid-1600s.

The hostility between the French and the Iroquois fluctuated. During a peaceful period in 1669, a team of explorers and priests, led by Rene-Robert Cavalier, Sieur de La Salle, passed through and noted the river and elevated ground that would eventually be the site of the fort. La Salle returned nine years later with the intention of establishing a ship-building business above Niagara Falls. In order to protect and supply his business, La Salle had a storehouse and stockade built in 1679. He named it Fort Conti, after Louis Armand de Bourbon, Prince of Conti. Fort Conti was short-lived. Several months after its construction careless guards accidentally burned it to the ground.

By 1687, tensions between the Iroquois and the French were high. The French waged battles against the Seneca Indians throughout the Genesee Valley, with limited success. Governor Denonville decided to build a fort near the site of Fort Conti, in an effort to strengthen the French position against the Iroquois. Fort Denonville consisted of eight buildings and a stockade. As winter approached, Captain Pierre de Troyes was left at the fort with a hundred men, while Denonville and others returned to Montreal.

Winter was brutal to de Troyes and his men. The harsh weather, deep freezes, and the Seneca Indians who surrounded them took a heavy toll. Starvation set in as the outpost was cut off from supplies and was beset by disease. The troops within were annihilated. By Good Friday 1688, when the relief force from Montreal arrived, only a dozen soldiers had survived, along with de Troyes, who was very ill.

The rescuers provided what comfort they could to the survivors. The Jesuit pastor with them, Father Pierre Millet, ordered a large wooden cross to be erected within the fort, and then performed Mass for the remaining soldiers. Shortly after the service, de Troyes took a turn for the worse, was given the last rites, and died in the arms of Father Millet.

The remaining soldiers were removed, and replacements arrived. The new troops were not expected to attempt to survive the winter this time: The army had learned its lesson. Instead, in September 1688, the soldiers evacuated for winter and did not return.

Between the French retreat from Fort Denonville and their return thirty-eight years later, much changed in the region. Most notably, the English had taken control of New York (formerly Nieuw Amsterdam) from the Dutch. The English, as they took control of the region, also inherited the Dutch alliance with the Five Nations, again leaving the French at odds with the Native Americans. Both powers, English and French, were striving for control of America.

Around the turn of the eighteenth century, the French began a campaign of improving relations with the Iroquois, especially the Seneca. They forged a relationship with the Indians through fur traders, who communicated regularly with the Seneca. In 1720, the Iroquois grudgingly permitted Louis-Thomas Chabert de Joncaire to build a trading post near the site of the previous forts. The Indians were reluctant to allow any military encroachment on the area, but were reassured that the post would be a trading post, and not a military establishment. De Joncaire named the new post "Magazin Royale," and began trading with the Indians. The English eyed his French flag warily, displeased at this trespass across Lake Ontario.

The trading post was not viewed as a significant threat to the British, who largely ignored it. However, behind the scenes, Chabert de Joncaire began to increase his holdings. The Iroquois granted permission for the trading post to expand in 1725. By 1726, the French arrived in ships to construct a new post at the site of the old Fort Denonville. De Joncaire called his larger trading post "House of Peace" to allay the suspicions of the Iroquois, who at that time were neutral toward both the British and the French.

Taking pains not to appear to be building a military fort, the French constructed a stone house with overhanging dormers on the second floor, surrounded by a stockade. The French referred to this larger trading post as the French Castle, but were careful to always refer to it as the "House of Peace" to the Iroquois.

In completing the French Castle, the French had made a significant move in solidifying their claim in America. Although the British were able to access Lake Ontario via the Oswego River, and had built a fort there, the House of Peace presented a significant barrier to their access to any of the other Great Lakes.

The value of the French holding at the site became evident as years passed. King George's War (1744–1748) made the French realize that their site at the portage around the falls, as well as the gateway to the Great Lakes, was an important one. They resolved to improve the strength of the post.

After the end of King George's War, the French fortified the House of Peace. They expanded the old stockade, adding new pickets. Within the larger open space, the French built several new buildings for housing soldiers and storing munitions. It became more and more obvious that the House of Peace was becoming a strategic military site, as the French prepared to encroach further into English-held New York and the rest of the wilds of the New World. The House of Peace became known as Fort Niagara.

The French began using Fort Niagara as a base of operations. Celeron de Blainville left from the fort to claim French possession of the Lake Erie region. The British contested the French claim on a fort at the site of modern-day Pittsburgh. Fighting subsequently broke out, which began the French and Indian War.

It was soon obvious to the French that the current stockade fence at Fort Niagara, while effective against small arms, would not withstand cannon fire, which was surely coming, now that the war had begun. Meanwhile, British troops were gathering at Fort Oswego, making plans for invading Fort Niagara. Had they followed through at that time, they likely would have overcome the weak defenses at Fort Niagara, changing the course of the war. However, British general William Shirley waited too long. Soon autumn was approaching, and Shirley decided to wait until spring to attack. His delay allowed the French the valuable time to significantly enlarge the fort, build huge earthenwork defenses, and to stock it with men and munitions. Fortunately for the French, General Shirley never did attack, as Fort Oswego fell in 1756.

By this time the Five Nations of the Iroquois were now Six Nations, having accepted the Tuscarora into their league. They had tried to remain neutral, but began to view the English as the likely victors in the war, and thus the best to ally with. British Indian superintendent Sir William Johnson finally persuaded the Iroquois to ally with the British in 1758.

Expecting an attack, French captain Pouchot arrived at Niagara, with plans to hold the fort. On July 6, 1759, Sir Johnson led a contingent of 2,000 soldiers and 1,500 Iroquois warriors to lay siege to Fort Niagara. The siege lasted nineteen days. The British dug trenches toward the fort walls, built shelters for their heavy artillery, and slowly advanced upon the French. They fired volley after volley of heavy munitions at Fort Niagara. Captain Pouchot held on, hoping the reinforcements he had requested would arrive in time to save Fort Niagara.

On July 6, 1759, 1,500 Frenchmen and Indian allies arrived, hoping to cut through the British and get to the fort. Johnson was prepared for them and blocked the road. The French attacked, but within twenty minutes were defeated. The French rescuers retreated back to Lake Erie. Upon hearing of this, Captain Pouchot surrendered. On July 25, 1759, the Union Jack was raised over Fort Niagara.

The British takeover of Fort Niagara cut the supply line between the French in America and their home bases in Canada. However, the British troops' months at the fort were not the triumphant tenure they had hoped for. While a critical strategic site, the fort was very difficult for the English to resupply. Their supply route ran from New York City up the Mohawk Valley to Lake Ontario, and then west to Fort Niagara. A scurvy epidemic broke out at Niagara as a result of poor nutrition, and by spring 1760, 150 men had died from the disease. By the fall of 1760, however, the British had adequately supplied the fort, and it became a critical post, allowing the British to dominate the Great Lakes.

One obstacle that the British experienced as the victors and the stewards of the Great Lakes was their troubled relations with the native people. While some of the local Indians had been allies of the British, others had allied with the French during the war, and were displeased to find themselves suddenly living on British soil.

Sir William Johnson had long been friendly with most of the Great Lakes Indians. He held a summit in 1761 at Fort Niagara with the chiefs of the lake tribes. At the end of the council meeting, another uneasy alliance had formed. However, many British traders and officials insisted upon treating the Native Americans as inferiors, frequently insulting them. The alliance quickly began to break down.

By the spring of 1763, the native tribes were at war with the British. Eight military posts had already been taken, leaving only Detroit and Fort Pitt. Fort Niagara was critical in helping to resupply Detroit while it was besieged, allowing it to withstand the siege. The Indians realized that Fort Niagara was preventing their success and turned their attention to attacking it.

A group of Seneca Indians, many of whom came from Little Beard's Town (see page 131), attacked a line of horses and wagons near "Devil's Hole" outside the fort's perimeter on September 14, 1763. The Indians also ambushed the soldiers racing to the wagon train's rescue, causing the most costly British defeat in the war. The attack led to an interruption in supply efforts for Detroit.

The British realized that decisively ending the war with the Indians was critical. In the summer of 1764, Johnson held a huge council for the various tribes. The tribes who chose not to attend were deemed enemies and risked retaliation, and the tribes who did attend were expected to remain friendly.

With the French effectively removed to Canada, the British no longer felt the need to keep the heavy fortifications at Niagara. The Native Americans lacked the French's heavy firepower. The condition of the fort's defenses began to deteriorate. The British were careful to maintain the wooden picketing, which protected them from attacks from Indians, however. By 1775, the heavy fortifications and earthenworks had fallen into significant disrepair. The British at Niagara were unprepared for the coming storm.

As the American colonists began to revolt against British rule, the British at Fort Niagara found themselves in the same strategic position that the French had been in years previously: controller of access to the Great Lakes. Niagara became a base of operations for colonial loyalists and Native American allies.

John Butler led many raids from Fort Niagara. His regiment, "Butler's Rangers," consisted of loyalists and Native Americans. They struck terror in the hearts of the frontier residents. The Rangers committed many atrocities during their attacks on the settlers, which served to stir the Americans to outrage and escalate the conflict.

In retaliation, the American army mobilized under General John Sullivan and marched toward Fort Niagara. The British panicked, realizing that their dilapidated defenses might not be adequate to ward off the attack. They scrambled to repair the defenses and stock the fort with supplies in advance of the expected siege.

Sullivan, in reality, had no intention of attacking Fort Niagara. Instead, he focused on destroying Iroquois villages, crops, and orchards before returning to Pennsylvania. The Native Americans, realizing that they might not survive the winter with their crops ruined, appeared at the fort as refugees, straining the fort's resources. Within several months, however, the British had recovered their equilibrium, and resumed their attacks on the settlers.

When the War for Independence ended, the Treaty of Paris drew the boundary between the United States and Canada through the Great Lakes, meaning that Fort Niagara now belonged to the Americans. It also meant that the Iroquois were now living solidly within the boundaries of the United States, with whom they had been at war. The British disputed the terms of the treaty and retained control of the fort for over a decade before finally transferring the fort to the Americans in August 1796.

The area around the fort became more populated, and towns began to spring up. Meanwhile, the British constructed their own forts across the water from Niagara. Fort George, in particular, was a direct threat to Niagara, and its elevation allowed it to fire somewhat downward onto the opposing fort.

By the time the War of 1812 broke out, Fort Niagara was again unprepared. Fortunately, the British in Fort George were equally ill prepared. Regiments from both sides struggled to quickly train troops and strengthen defenses.

On November 21, 1812, the hard work paid off. British Fort George opened fire on Fort Niagara. But the cannons that the Americans had mounted on top of the French Castle were a solid match for the elevated position of Fort George. At one point, an American soldier was killed as he loaded his cannon. Without hesitation, a fellow soldier's wife, Betsy Doyle, stepped up and began loading the cannon. Her courage heartened the men, who claimed victory over the British.

On the bitter cold night of December 18, 1813, over 550 British soldiers stole onto American soil, quietly killed the lookouts, and approached the fort. Unfortunately, the fort's commander, Captain Nathaniel Leonard, was not present, as he was visiting his family in Lewiston. The Americans were taken by surprise, and the British took the fort. When Leonard returned to the fort, he was met by British sentries. He was imprisoned in Canada, which is the only reason he escaped being arrested by the Americans for treason. When the Treaty of Ghent ended the war in late 1814, the fort was returned to the Americans. Peaceful times followed for several years.

When the Erie Canal was built in 1825, it eliminated the need for a portage on the Niagara River, one of the main strategic reasons for Fort Niagara. Within a year, the fort was abandoned and placed in the hands of a caretaker.

A mysterious incident took place at the empty fort in 1826. William Morgan, a Freemason, had published information about the secrets of Freemasonry. The other Masons were enraged. On September 12, 1826, Morgan was abducted by Freemasons. He was transported to Fort Niagara, whose caretaker was also a Mason. The caretaker allowed the kidnappers to bring Morgan in, and he was imprisoned in the empty powder magazine. While Morgan awaited his fate, his kidnappers argued about whether to put him to death. When the abductors went to check on Morgan, he was gone. He was never heard from again.

The fort was manned off and on for the next few decades. The start of the Civil War saw the fort manned again—not for fear of Confederate troops marching to Niagara, but out of concern that the British might enter the war on the side of the Confederacy, and attack from Canada. Repairs were made to the weakened defenses, but as the South began to falter the British lost interest in entering the fray.

The holdings at Fort Niagara continued to be slowly improved and expanded. A thousand-yard rifle range was built. In part because of the rifle range, the fort was used increasingly as a training facility. Following the Spanish-American War, the fort was used to train troops recruited for service in the Philippines, and later for troops training for World War I.

Over time, the age of the fort began to show. Buildings were crumbling, and the seawall was falling apart. Local citizens formed the Old Fort Niagara Association in 1927, intending to restore the fort as a museum. During the restoration, the fort remained staffed with soldiers, who helped with the construction work.

In 1944, after World War II broke out, a section of Fort Niagara was fenced as a prisoner of war camp. Some of General Erwin Rommel's Afrika Corps were held there. The prisoners worked on local farms, under guard. The camp was closed in 1946. The end of Fort Niagara's life as a fort finally came in 1963, when the U.S. Army deeded the site to the State of New York.

The Town Today

Fort Niagara stands as a restored fort, with a visitor's center, and many original and restored buildings open to the public. It is open to visitors all year. Reenactments are held, and educational programs are available. Admission is charged.

Directions

From the NYS Thruway, take Exit 50. Follow I-290 West to I-190. Take I-190 North to Exit 25B. Follow Robert Moses Parkway north to the fort.

LOVE CANAL

The site of one of America's most devastating toxic waste tragedies, Love Canal was a cautionary tale for many chemical manufacturers.

History

Love Canal's name suggests a happy place, full of joyful couples holding hands as they skip through daisy-filled meadows. The reality is very different.

In 1892, a man named William T. Love speculated that connecting the upper and lower Niagara River would create a 280-foot manmade waterfall that could provide a cheap source of power. This connector was intended to be six miles long, but excavation was halted when funding dried up. The partially completed canal was three thousand feet long, ten feet deep, and sixty feet wide. The locals enjoyed swimming and fishing in it. In 1920, the land was sold to Elon Huntington Hooker, who owned the Hooker Electrochemical Company, for use as a municipal and chemical disposal site. Mr. Hooker planned to use the site to bury byproducts from his chemical manufacturing.

At that time, burying chemical waste was acceptable. There were no zoning regulations to prevent companies from burying toxic waste near neighborhoods or schools. Little research existed on the dangers that proximity to toxic chemicals can have on the human body. There were no laws dictating the proper disposal of chemical or hazardous waste, or of mitigating the damage to the environment done by the waste.

The Hooker Electrochemical Company (later known as the Hooker Chemical Company) manufactured various pesticides, plastics, fertilizers, and industrial chemicals. Two of the most critical items that Hooker Chemical manufactured were chlorine and caustic soda. Caustic soda, also known as sodium hydroxide, is often used in the aluminum, paper, and petroleum industries. The waste from production included chlorobenzenes, which can cause cancer and blood disorders; these chemicals were present in approximately four million pounds of the waste. Dioxin comprised another several hundred pounds. Dioxin, a strong weed killer, can cause cancer, nerve damage, and several other diseases.

The U.S. Army reportedly dumped possible chemical warfare byproducts and even items related to the Manhattan Project at the site. The government denies this.

From 1942 to 1953, the chemicals were sealed in metal drums, placed in the canal, and covered with a layer of clay. It was believed that the clay would serve as a sort of seal, preventing water from seeping in and damaging the barrels. After 42 million pounds of dangerous chemicals were buried, the company was out of room in the canal.

Thinking that the site was effectively sealed, the Hooker Corporation sold the site to the City of Niagara Board of Education for one dollar. Hooker Chemical took a hefty tax write-off in the process. In the deed, Hooker had included a warning about the poisonous chemicals that were buried below the surface. The deed states that the canal "has been filled . . . with waste products resulting from the manufacturing of chemicals." The intent of the disclaimer was undoubtedly to protect the company from future litigation.

Within a year, the City of Niagara Falls began to build on the site. Roads, homes, and businesses were built. Most shocking, the 99th Street Elementary School, which served four hundred children, was built directly on top of the landfill. By 1978, there were over eight hundred homes and over two hundred low-income apartments on the site. Residents were not informed of the toxic chemicals buried beneath their homes.

In the 1960s residents in the area began to notice a smelly black oily substance leaching into their basements and yards. Puddles of it appeared on the school playground. The local children reportedly kept special shoes for playing in the "quicksand lagoon" on the playground, since shoes that touched the substances never could be cleaned. One child, Joey Bulka, fell into the "lagoon" one day in 1965. Some of the muddy liquid entered his ear canal and burned a hole in his eardrum. His parents complained to the school board and the local health department, but nothing was done.

Other problems were appearing as well. Residents had difficulty growing lawns or gardens. The few vegetables that grew were very hard, and had odd shapes. Locals started noticing strange rashes and burns on their skin.

City inspectors responded to the complaints, but very little was done to address the problem. When the ooze was observed on school property, it was covered with soil.

In 1977, Calspan Corporation was brought in to investigate the complaints. Their report stated that there was toxic residue in the air in the area, and that people on the south end of the canal had dangerous chemicals in their sump pumps. The report also noted that several of the metal barrels containing the toxic chemicals had risen to just below the clay barrier. The local storm sewer contained dangerously high levels of PCBs (polychlorinated biphenyls).

Calspan recommended covering the canal with another clay cap, initiating a new, extensive drainage system to control where waste water traveled, and sealing residential sump pumps. Unfortunately, none of the recommendations were taken.

Rumbling about the chemicals continued throughout the area. On October 3, 1976, the *Niagara Gazette* broke the story. The newspaper reported about the seepage of chemicals, as well as illnesses in residents and animals in the area. On November 2, 1976, the newspaper catalogued the chemical analysis of the leaching substance. Readers were horrified about the dangerous nature of the chemicals entering basements, water, soil, and the air in the area.

Thanks to the increasing attention of the media and outcry of the residents, the Environmental Protection Agency (EPA) investigated. Their October 8, 1977, report was shocking. The barrels in the landfill were rusting and full of holes. Homes in the area had noxious seepage standing in their basements, which ate into wooden structures and corroded paint. The smell could be overwhelming. Clothing kept the odor even after multiple washings.

On August 2, 1978, Dr. Robert Whalen, the New York State Comissioner of Health, declared a medical emergency at Love Canal. On August 7, 1978, the federal government followed suit, as President Jimmy Carter declared Love Canal a federal emergency.

In 1979, a study was published that asserted that the Love Canal residents had higher-than-normal rates of birth defects and miscarriages. The local children had statistically more learning disabilities, seizure disorders, and other health issues.

The federal government gave New York $20 million to relocate 239 affected families. The residents living directly above the contaminated site were relocated first, followed by those within increasingly distant perimeters outside the initial contamination zone.

Hooker Chemical, despite its attempt to protect itself from liability in the deed to the land, found itself besieged by lawsuits. It ultimately changed its name to Occidental Chemical because of the negative publicity associated with its name. In the end, the United States government settled with Occidental Chemical for $129 million to cover cleanup, relocation, and interest.

The Town Today

Little remains of Love Canal today. The actual site is now a field surrounded by a chain-link fence. In the 1990s, parts of the site were deemed safe to inhabit again, and homes have been sold there. One such neighborhood is on the north portion of the site. It has been named "Black Creek Village."

Directions

From Buffalo, take I-190N toward the Peace Bridge/Canada. Take Exit 21A onto the Lasalle Expressway East. Merge onto Buffalo Ave/Route 384S. Turn left onto 102nd street. Take the first left onto Frontier Avenue. Take the second right onto 100th Street to the site.

RICHBURG

A town now exists where this oil boomtown once stood, but it bears little resemblance to the "lively and wicked" place it once was.

History

Before oil was discovered in the area, Richburg was a tiny village of approximately twenty-five homes along the main road. It was populated mostly by farmers, all of whom were unaware of the potential wealth beneath their feet.

After oil was discovered south of Richburg near Titusville, Pennsylvania, speculators began to spread out in search of more oil. Several test wells were drilled in Allegany County, New York, but little oil was located. On the morning of April 27, 1881, everything changed. A well known as the Boyle Well was drilled on a hill near Richburg. Unlike the others, it started pumping a significant amount of oil. Within a short time, it was pumping four hundred barrels a day of rich crude. A boomtown was born. By the next day, thanks to word spreading by telegraph, people began flocking to the area. Speculators raced to secure leases in the Richburg area. The town's population exploded with men looking to get rich. Stagecoach lines were established within days.

To accommodate the influx of people, many hotels, houses, taverns, and dance halls appeared overnight. Such hastily built structures tended to be poorly made, but the speculators did not care. Despite the building boom, there were far too few accommodations for the men. Saloon owners began charging tired speculators a dollar a night to sleep on a billiard table, or fifty cents to sleep in a bar chair. Men would sleep in hay piles in barns, or under trees in the town park.

Leases, when they were available, could be purchased for approximately $50 a month for a lot measuring approximately twenty feet long. The leases were snapped up quickly, and many walked away disappointed. Speculators drilled wherever they could. Garden plots and the local cemetery were not immune to oil fever.

Even the local church got in on the action by investing some of its funds in oil speculation.

Crime flourished in the boomtown as the freely flowing cash drew criminals of various degrees. Holdups and personal robberies were a daily occurrence. When farmers brought wagons of produce to the town, they hired gunmen to accompany them to avoid being robbed. Murders were common. One such murder was committed in November 1881, in front of many eyewitnesses. John O. McCarthy, a career criminal on the run from the law, without warning, stabbed Patrick Markey in front of a saloon. The enraged crowd attempted to exact some frontier justice, but McCarthy's life was saved by police officers. He was hanged the following March in Angelica, New York.

At its peak, Richburg had over a hundred saloons—few, if any, licensed to sell alcohol. The demand for alcohol from the oilmen was very high. One entrepreneur was building his saloon when his liquor stock arrived. Refusing to lose a day's income, he set up a makeshift bar by placing a plank on two whisky barrels. He made $72 the first day, even without his saloon officially being open for business.

Besides the shoddily-made boomtown structures, Richburg also had some more established buildings. Two banks handled the business deposits for the town. An opera house provided highbrow entertainment. There were two fire companies, a high school, and a brick church. There were also some established non-oil businesses, such as machine shops and two daily newspapers.

By May of 1882, the oil fields in Pennsylvania were booming, with larger gushers than New York state had. Richburg's speculators began to drift south to Pennsylvania, and to nearby Bolivar. The boomtown had ended. Fires destroyed many of the buildings in town, and others were torn down and relocated to other towns. The opera house was converted into a cheese factory.

The Town Today

Richburg still exists, although it does not resemble the wild boomtown of 1881. The Pioneer Oil Museum in nearby Bolivar keeps the history of this small town alive. It is managed by friendly, knowledgeable staff, but keeps variable hours. Please contact them before visiting. In 1939, a monument was erected at the site of the first Richburg oil well.

Directions

To reach the Richburg Oil Well monument, take Route 275 north from Bolivar. Pass the cemetery on the left, which is worth a visit. Turn right on Depot Road Drive and go .9 miles to reach the monument. Please note that Depot Road is in poor conditions in places, and is a dirt road for much of the drive. In poor weather, it can be a difficult drive.

ST. HELENA

The raw natural beauty of this area is surpassed only by the story of the amazing woman who owned the land for many years.

History

The story of St. Helena cannot be fully told without telling the remarkable story of Mary Jemison. Mary Jemison was born on the ship *William and Mary*, bound for Philadelphia from Ireland, in 1743. Her family settled on land on Marsh Creek, on the outskirts of present-day Gettysburg, Pennsylvania. Mary was one of six children born to Thomas and Jane Jemison.

In the early 1750s, stories of Indian atrocities against settlers began to circulate in the area. The Jemisons feared for the safety of their children. Besides the murders, the stories of the hideous tortures visited upon surviving captives terrified the settlers.

On a spring day in 1755, Mary's father was planting flax in the field with two of his sons. Mary had been sent the evening before to a neighbor's farm to borrow a horse. Feeling ill, she had spent the night at the neighbor's house and returned home very early in the morning. When she arrived home, there were visitors at the house. As the men left to go about their business, the women started to make breakfast and catch up on the local gossip.

The sound of gunshots nearby shocked the women. They opened the door of the cabin to find the male visitor and his horse lying dead several feet away. Mary Jemison later learned that the man had unknowingly been pursued by the Indians from his own home to the Jemisons' house.

The marauding Indians secured Mary's father and then entered the house. Within moments, and with no struggle, Mary, her mother, her brothers, and her sisters, along the visiting woman and her three children, were captured. The attacking group consisted of six Indians and four Frenchmen. They looted the home, focusing mostly on provisions such as flour, bread, and meat. They then set out in haste with their captives.

They marched through the woods all day, with one of the Indians brandishing a whip, striking the captives whenever they slowed down. They were given nothing to eat or drink. If any of the children cried with thirst, the Indians told them no, or made them drink their own urine. They slept that night on the ground, with no relief from hunger or thirst. Again the next day they were forced to march. After several hours, they were given breakfast, consisting of food stolen from the Jemison house. Most of the captives, ravenous, ate quickly. Mr. Jemison, however, had lapsed into a kind of stupor or despair and was unable to eat or drink. But Mary's mother was strong and tough, and was determined to keep her children alive.

After dinner on the second day, one of the Indians approached Mary and removed her shoes and stockings. He then replaced them with a pair of moccasins. Mary's mother correctly interpreted the Indian's actions, and realized that there was hope that her daughter would survive the ordeal.

Her mother spoke quietly and vehemently to Mary. She told Mary that most of the captives were likely to be murdered shortly, but that Mary would likely survive. She told Mary to always remember the names of her parents, and to remember how to speak English. She warned Mary not to attempt to escape, even if the opportunity presented itself. She assured Mary that an escape attempt would be grounds for the Indians to murder her.

As Mary's mother spoke to her, the Indians also placed moccasins on the feet of a little boy belonging to the family who had been visiting. An Indian took both Mary and the little boy by their hands and led them away into the woods. After a while, the three lay down for the night. During the night, the little boy begged Mary to run away with him while their Indian captor was sleeping, but she refused, remembering her mother's warning.

The next morning, the rest of the war party caught up with them, but no other prisoners were with them. Mary was devastated, but she was wary about angering the Indians. She held her emotions in check, only allowing herself to sob quietly. She later learned that all of the other captives had been murdered and scalped and left for wild animals. After a quick breakfast, the much smaller group rushed on, with one Indian trailing behind. The last man used a long stick to push bent-over grass back upright, completely erasing their trail.

At dinner that day, the Indians removed the scalps of the captives from their packs, and proceeded to prepare and preserve them. They scraped the flesh from them, and then spread them, still wet and bloody, to dry by the fire. Mary was able to easily identify her own mother's scalp by her lovely red hair, but she again behaved stoically. However, the Indians sensed her distress, and communicated with her that, had white settlers not been following them, they would not have been forced to kill their captives.

Indeed, Mary learned years later that her neighbors had been following the group. They came upon the bodies of the murdered captives, and were appalled at the brutality of the murders. They realized that Mary and the other little boy were not among the dead, but the Indians had covered their trail so thoroughly that they were unable to determine which direction they had gone.

After several days of marching through rain and snow, the group arrived at Fort du Quesne (later named Fort Pitt), which was then occupied by the French. Before entering the fort, the Indians combed their captives' hair and painted their faces red. They then entered the fort, placed the captives in an empty house, and locked them in.

In the morning, the little boy and another male captive who had joined them on the trail were handed over to the French and were taken away. Later in the day, two Indian women came to examine Mary as she shivered alone in the abandoned house. The women looked Mary over carefully, and then left. They returned a short time later with Mary's captors, who then gave Mary to the women. The women, the captors, and Mary left on canoes down the Ohio River. One of the original captors brought out the scalps of Mary's family and friends and hung them from a pole in the canoe.

After they arrived at their village, the women clothed Mary in clean new Indian clothes, and made her comfortable in their long-house. Mary later learned that she had been given to the women to compensate for their brother, who had been killed by whites. The women could choose to adopt Mary or torture and kill her, depend-ing on their wishes. Fortunately, the women decided to adopt her.

The women were very kind to Mary. She helped around the long-house and village and assisted in childcare for the various families living there. Although the two sisters who had adopted Mary had forbidden her to speak English, Mary recited catechism, prayers, and other things that she had memorized when she was alone. In this way, she remembered how to speak English.

The following year, Mary and the village traveled to Fort Pitt to make peace with the British, who now controlled it. The British were very interested in Mary, inquiring about her name, parents, and so on. The sisters, fearing that Mary would be taken from them, fled back to the Indian village with her. Mary later learned that the British had, indeed, made a significant but unsuccessful effort to find her and secure her return.

After several essentially content years with the sisters, Mary was informed that she was to be married to a Delaware Indian, Sheninjee, whom Mary had not met. Luckily, he was a noble, kind, generous man, and Mary came to love him. She gave birth to a little girl who died, and a little boy she named Thomas Jefferson after her father.

When her son was several months old, Mary traveled to Little Beard's Town (see page 131), in New York. Little Beard's Town, also known as Genishau, was then a huge Seneca town. While at Little Beard's Town, Mary received the sad news that, back in their village, her husband had fallen sick and died.

Two years later, the king of England offered a reward to anyone who would bring back prisoners of war and deposit them at military posts. A Dutchman, Jon Van Sice, wished to take Mary to Fort Niagara, but she refused. He attempted to kidnap her, but she hid. The Indian chiefs held a council, and decided that it was Mary's choice: Since she wanted to stay, she would be allowed to.

When her son was approximately four years old, Mary remarried. Her second husband's name was Hiokatoo, or Gardeau, and they became parents of four daughters and two sons. Hiokatoo was much older than Mary and was apparently very kind to her throughout her life.

At times, Mary's family hosted the famous Indian warrior Joseph Brant (mentioned in the Old Stone Fort chapter in this book, see page 35) in their home while he was in town. She often provided him with clothing and other provisions for his journeys.

During the Revolutionary War, Little Beard's Town was attacked and destroyed by General John Sullivan, a colonial officer, and his powerful army. Mary and the other Indians returned to their ruined town, but Mary saw little reason to stay. Not long after the end of the Revolutionary War, Mary's adoptive brother offered her her freedom. She considered it this time, especially as her son Thomas wanted to leave with her. The chiefs of the tribe, however, had seen leadership traits within Thomas that would make him a great warrior. They permitted Mary to leave, but under no circumstances would they allow Thomas to leave. Mary was very close to her son, and could not bear to leave him.

The other reason that swayed Mary's decision was her younger children. She knew that they would likely be treated poorly by white society. Mary told her brother that she intended to stay. Her brother was overjoyed by her decision and spoke to the great chiefs at

Buffalo about gifting Mary with a tract of land upon which she could peacefully live out her life.

Several years later, her petition for land was granted. The grant consisted of a tract of land along the Genesee River. More than six miles long and over four and a half miles wide, it encompassed 17,927 acres. The land was afterward known as the Gardeau Tract. St. Helena became a small village within the tract.

In 1810, Mary was told that a white cousin, George Jemison, had surfaced. He had fallen on very hard times, so she asked him and his family to come to her land, and live in one of the houses. After approximately seven years, Jemison asked Mary to deed him some of her land. Mary agreed, but when she asked to wait until a friend was available to help her with the legalities, Jemison became upset and tried to rush the deal. Mary was assured that she was only signing forty acres to Jemison, and so she signed the papers. In reality, she was deeding him 400 acres. Eventually Mary retrieved her land, and Jemison moved away, but she chafed under the fraud. By the end of her life, Mary was convinced that George Jemison was not a relative at all, but a con man.

Mary lived quietly with her family on her land for years. The peace came to an end on July 1, 1811, when her son John murdered his brother Thomas, who was drunk at the time, during an argument. John, fearing the consequences, fled to Canada, although he returned when the council of chiefs determined that the killing had been justified. Mary's husband, Hiokatoo, died in November of the same year, at the age of 103.

In May 1812, another of Mary's sons murdered another, and again alcohol was a significant factor. Mary suffered greatly from these losses and the murder of another of her children some time later.

In 1831, Mary sold off her land and moved to the Buffalo Creek Reservation to spend her last days among her Indian friends. She died there on September 19, 1833, at approximately 91 years of age. She was initially buried near Buffalo. Her grandson later had her exhumed and reburied near the upper falls of the Genesee River, a place that Mary had loved.

St. Helena was initially populated with squatters who were apparently tolerated by Mary and her family. In 1823, Mary sold the tract of land including St. Helena to her friends Micah Brooks, Jellis Clute, and Henry Gibson. In 1835, families began to formally move into the town, anticipating the mills that eventually sprang up along the Genesee River. A covered bridge was built across the river at St. Helena. By 1860, St. Helena was a successful, prosperous town, boasting a flour mill, a shingle mill, a paper mill, two sawmills, a school, several stores, a hotel, and at least twenty-five homes.

In 1867, a mill fire put many residents out of work, and the federal government ended the post office at St. Helena. The Genesee River's ice took out the vital bridge in 1884. It took two years for the bridge to be replaced, but the new bridge was also destroyed by ice in 1904. An iron bridge replaced the second bridge, but by then the town's days were numbered.

Floods and a lack of business opportunities eroded the town. The last family moved away in 1948. The iron bridge lasted until 1950. The ninety-two graves in the town's cemetery were moved in 1952 to a section of the Grace Cemetery in nearby Castile.

The Town Today

St. Helena is located inside what is now Letchworth State Park. There is almost nothing left of the town. The only obvious marker is a sign reading "St. Helena" at the picnic area. The bridge abutments are visible, but the bridge is long gone. Few foundations are evident.

Although little remains of St. Helena, there are significant remnants of the remarkable woman whose land on which the town stood. Information about Mary Jemison is available at the park ranger station. A short trail behind the museum leads to a statue of Mary, depicting her during the walk to Little Beard's Town with Thomas on her back, looking out over the beautiful valley in the park. If you look very carefully, you can find the small etching of a wolf head that the sculptor hid on the statue. Mary's cabin and grave, as well as a Seneca council house, are located near the statue.

It should be noted that Letchworth State Park, despite the lack of remains of St. Helena, is well worth the trip. Besides the Mary Jemison artifacts, the park encompasses some of the most awesome gorges and hiking trails in New York State. Picnic tables and other recreational facilities are available in the park.

Directions

From the Buffalo area, take U.S. Route 20A toward East Aurora. Turn right onto Mt. Morris Road/Route 36. Turn right onto Chapel Street/Route 408. Turn right onto Park Road. Passing the visitor center, stay left, and the St. Helena picnic area will be on your left. Past the town, signs guide you to the museum, statue, and other attractions.

LITTLE BEARD'S TOWN

Once a powerful Seneca village, Little Beard's Town was home to some of the most famous Native American historical figures.

History

Little Beard's Town, also known as Genishau, or Genesee, was one of the largest Seneca villages. It was located where current Cuylerville, New York, now stands.

Mary Jemison, the "White Woman of the Genesee," lived for several years at Little Beard's Town. Jemison, whose life was related in the previous chapter, had been captured as a young teenage girl from the Gettysburg, Pennsylvania, area in 1755. She was initially taken to the Pittsburgh area, and then Ohio, where she lived in peace with her adopted Indian family. She married a young Seneca man, Sheninjee, with whom she had a son, Thomas.

When Thomas was approximately three months old, Mary accepted an invitation to visit her Seneca relatives in Little Beard's Town. She traveled with her adopted brothers, and her husband planned to join her later. Unfortunately, she received word that he had died of an illness before he could travel to New York.

The town was situated on the shoreline of the Genesee River. Many Indian places and people had multiple names, and Little Beard's Town was also known as Deonundagaa, which translates to "where the hill is near." Although there were several other Seneca towns in the area, Little Beard's Town was by far the largest.

The town's namesake, Little Beard, was a tough leader. History remembers Little Beard as somewhat tyrannical. He was strong and forceful, but could also be cruel and arbitrary in his moods and decisions.

Records were not kept for Indian villages the way they were in white communities, so it is not known exactly when the town began, or how extensive it was. Some records suggest that there were 120 to 130 homes, with extensive fields growing every imaginable vegetable. It was viewed as a very prosperous town among the Native Americans.

The houses were fairly large, with space for visitors. They were also designed to be easily dismantled if necessary. They were built from hickory sapling frames covered with strips of linden bark. The houses had windows that also served as chimneys, as many of the houses had fireplaces within. Inside, there were beds or bunks with deerskin bedding; the families stored firewood and supplies under the beds. During the winter, family members often slept together around the hearth for warmth.

When Mary Jemison arrived at Little Beard's Town, the residents were making preparations to ally themselves with the French. The French were intending to attempt to retake Fort Niagara (or, as the Senecas called it, Ne-a-gau). A group of French and Seneca set out from Little Beard's Town toward Fort Niagara in full war dress. Meanwhile, the British at the fort had sent out a group of soldiers to attempt to take Fort Schlosser, not far from Niagara. They expected an easy victory, so the contingent was rather small. The French and Indians lay in wait and ambushed the British, devastating the group. They returned to Little Beard's Town several days later with two

British soldiers and several oxen, which were the first cattle to be seen in the village.

The British soldiers endured unspeakable torture in Little Beard's Town, as the Indians feasted and celebrated. The soldiers were ultimately executed, dismembered, and burnt to ashes on the other side of the Genesee River. Men from Little Beard's Town also were part of the contingent who drove the British off Devil's Hole (see "Fort Niagara," page 109).

For approximately a dozen years after the conclusion of the French and Indian War, the Seneca Nation enjoyed a period of peace. When the Revolutionary War began, the leadership of Little Beard's Town, along with other Seneca leadership, met at a council to decide which side they would support. The Senecas decided to remain resolutely neutral. In time, however, a message arrived at Little Beard's Town from the British military leaders, asking for their presence at Fort Oswego. At first the Senecas refused, referring to their decision for neutrality from the year before.

However, the British persuaded the Seneca by convincing them that the colonists were weak and would be easily conquered. For their help, the British king would reward the Seneca richly. The Indians agreed and signed a treaty with the British. On signing, each Indian was given a uniform, a scalping knife, a gun, a brass pot, gunpowder, and a promise of a reward for each colonial scalp they brought back.

During the American Revolution, Mary Jemison and her family hosted both Colonel Walter Butler and Colonel Joseph Brant when they were in Little Beard's Town. Joseph Brant, or Thayendanegea, was a brilliant Mohawk leader. He was educated, thoughtful, and highly intelligent. Colonel Butler's father, John Butler, had been the leader of Butler's Rangers, which Walter joined. The two men were instrumental in the Cherry Valley Massacre on November 11, 1788, along with others from Little Beard's Town.

The attack by British and Indians on Cherry Valley became known as one of the most horrific massacres of the war. Especially appalling was the intentional targeting of noncombatants, including

women and children, by the Indians. Reports stated that thirty inno-
cents were murdered, along with many armed defenders.

Brant was accused of atrocities at Cherry Valley (as well as in
another battle, at which he was not even present). However, it is
reported that he attempted to intervene and stop the atrocities
against civilians at Cherry Valley.

The warriors returned to Little Beard's Town, believing themselves
victorious, with only five wounded warriors among them. Before
long, however, word spread of the brutality against the people of
Cherry Valley, and plans were made among the colonials for reprisals.

Major General John Sullivan, a colonial leader, was assigned to
seek revenge for the atrocities. His scorched-earth policy devastated
forty Indian villages throughout the Finger Lakes area, including Little Beard's Town. The town was utterly devastated, with houses,
crops, and fruit trees destroyed. The inhabitants fled to the Niagara
Falls region, and although many later returned, there was little left of
the town. Mary Jemison, among others, moved on to other lands.
The town never regained its place as a significant Seneca town.

The Town Today

Unfortunately, little remains of Little Beard's Town. Native American towns were typically made to be moveable, and their buildings
were constructed of tree limbs and bark instead of rock and brick.
The current town of Cuylerville now stands on the site.

Directions

From Canandaigua, New York, take Route 20/5 west. Take I-390
south toward Corning. Turn right onto Route 20A (exit 8). Follow
Route 20A to Cuylerville. There is an interpretive sign at the site.

SODUS BAY PHALANX

A beautiful stretch of Lake Ontario shoreline hosted a failed Utopian
community.

History

Founded in 1844, the Sodus Bay Phalanx was based on the tenets of Fourierism. Fourierism was based on the social and moral views of Francois Marie Charles Fourier, a French philosopher. Although he was viewed as radical during his lifetime for his views on Utopian Socialism, some of his ideas continue to be relevant today. For example, he coined the term "feminism" in 1837.

Fourier believed that cooperation was the foundation of a successful society. He viewed poverty as the main reason for discord in society, and believed that a system of higher wages and a "minimum wage" for those unable to work would eradicate many societal problems. He believed that workers should be reimbursed based on their jobs, and that jobs should be assigned based on the interests of the individual. Jobs considered undesirable by most would be entitled to higher pay.

Fourier's goal was to create communities, which he called "phalanxes," that would follow his teachings. Because he believed that there were twelve common passions, resulting in 810 types of characters, he believed that an ideal phalanx would have exactly 1,620 people. He envisioned a world with six million phalanxes, ruled by an omniarch.

Fourier believed that children were able to contribute to society as early as age two or three. He believed that work involving noisy environments and the need for curiosity would be suitable for such children.

Fourier's views on sexuality and relationships were considered radical at the time. He believed that homosexuality was a personal preference. He also suggested creating card catalogs of the personality types of the members of phalanxes to help visitors find suitable partners for casual sex.

The Fourierism community at Sodus Bay purchased 1,400 acres along Lake Ontario that had formerly been a Shaker colony. They named it the Sodus Bay Phalanx, and had high hopes for a successful Utopian community. They were fortunate that the property already boasted a fine harbor area, a sawmill, various shops, a meetinghouse, and approximately twenty-five homes. In addition, the Shakers had also left behind established fruit orchards and gardens.

From the beginning, the community experienced difficulty. Initial attempts to sell members shares of the community fell far short of the goals. In response, the community leaders offered to sell the $35,000 shares with no initial down payment; instead, a down payment of $9,500 would be due in two years. The leadership also promised free room and board for one year to anyone who wished to join the community.

The generous offer caused a flood of people to descend upon Sodus Bay. While some were legitimate Fourierists, many were people down on their luck, drawn by the promise of expense-free living for one year. The true followers of Fourierism were overwhelmed by the nonbelievers, many of whom were unable or unwilling to perform the work required to maintain the community.

The colony was essentially out of money before the end of the first year. By the summer of 1844, there were 260 people crowded into Sodus Bay Phalanx, many of whom did not possess viable work skills or any work ethic. The overcrowding facilitated illness, and typhoid swept through the colony.

In addition to the financial issues and illness, infighting brought an end to the short-lived community. The religious liberals battled the evangelical Protestants about many issues, including whether or not members should work on the Sabbath and how the Sodus Bay children should be educated. Eventually the liberals won, and the evangelicals began to decamp. Most of the evangelical Protestants were gone by the spring of 1845. Their departure further eroded the stability of the community, which rapidly approached bankruptcy. Members continued to leave, often under cover of night, taking with them as much of the community's property as they could carry. In April of 1846, the thirteen remaining community members admitted defeat and dissolved the community.

The Town Today

The property was vacant until 1868 and then changed hands several times. It was most notably owned by the Strong family in the early twentieth century, during which time it was named Alasa Farms. It currently is owned by an organization named Cracker Box Palace, which uses the property to care for farm animals recovering from abuse or neglect.

The Main House, Deacons House, three gambrel-roofed frame barns, the board and batten barn, the pony barn, the granary, the farmhand house, the in-ground pool and pool house, and the tenant house are still standing. The property is available for tours. Contact the Cracker Box Palace organization for details.

Directions

From Rochester, take Route 590 north to Route 104 east. Take Route 104 for 30.3 miles. Turn right onto Route 14. Turn right onto Red Mill Road. Turn right onto Shaker Road The site's address is 6450 Shaker Road, Alton, New York.

RED HOUSE

Records for this tiny hamlet are rare, but rumors that it is haunted persist. Explore if you dare!

History

The area that became Red House was first settled in 1828, by Darius Frink of Sterling, Connecticut. He located his home near the Little Red House Creek. His son built a home on Big Red House Creek, not far away. More settlers arrived. For some time, they considered themselves part of the town of Salamanca, a short distance away. Red House became its own entity on November 23, 1869.

The town was named for the Red House Creek, on which it was situated. The creek, in turn, was named after a house that stood at the Allegheny River, at the mouth of the creek. The house was painted dark red and served as a landmark for the raftsmen who navigated the river. The house was rumored to be haunted.

At its height, Red House had seven sawmills in operation, along with three shingle mills. Three schools for white children and one Indian school were within the town. In 1870, the population was 407, of whom forty were Native Americans.

One of the more prominent families in town was the Frecks family, for whom the town of Frecks is named. The story told is that the family lost their oldest son, Johnny, in the Civil War. His widow had an affair with his brother James that may or may not have begun before the death of her husband. The Frecks family was outraged by the lovers and rejected them. The lovers supposedly committed suicide together in the red house. The Frecks family lost the family patriarch shortly thereafter to a mysterious illness, and the family left town.

The Town Today

Like most lumber towns, depletion of the local woods took its toll on the town. Allegany State Park now owns much of the land of the town.

Directions

From the Southern Tier expressway, I-86/Route 17, take exit 20 toward Route 253/Salamanca. Turn right onto Route 417/Broad Street. Turn left onto Hoag Road/Old Route 17. The Red House town site is 4.2 miles ahead.

BIBLIOGRAPHY

Dunnigan, Brian. *A History and Guide to Old Fort Niagara*. Youngstown, NY: Old Fort Niagara Association, 2007.

Fitch, Jabez, Jr. *The Diary of Jabez Fitz, Jr. in the French and Indian War.* 1899. Reprint, Berkeley: University of California, 2007.

Gethard, Chris. *Weird New York*. New York: Sterling, 2005.

Gottlock, Wesley, and Barbara Gottlock. *Lost Towns of the Hudson Valley*. Charleston, SC: The History Press, 2009.

Guarneri, Carl. *The Utopian Alternative: Fourierism in Nineteenth Century America*. Ithaca, NY: Cornell University Press, 1991.

Hagan, Edward. *War in Schohary: 1777-1783*. Schoharie, NY: Tryon Press, 2010.

Hamilton, Edward. *Fort Ticonderoga: Key to a Continent*. Boston: Little, Brown, and Co., 1964.

Johnson, Thom, and Barbara Gottlock. *Bannerman Island*. Charleston, SC: Arcadia Publishing, 2006.

Klaw, Spencer. *Without Sin: The Life and Death of the Oneida Community*. New York: Penguin, 1993.

Lenski, Lois. *Indian Captive: The Story of Mary Jemison*. New York: HarperCollins, 1941, 1969.

Manchester, Lee, ed. *Tales from the Deserted Village: First Hand Accounts of Early Explorations into the Heart of the Adirondacks*. Self-published, 2010. PDF e-book.

Manko, Sandra. *Glimpses of Sharon Springs*. Sharon Springs, NY: Sharon Historical Society, 2006.

Manko, Sandra, and Jean Bakkom, eds. *A Touch of Nostalgia: Sharon Springs Spa*. Sharon Springs, NY: Sharon Historical Society, 2000.

Manko, Sandra, Katina Manko, and Jean Bakkom, eds. *Reflections on Sharon: 1797-1997, A Pictorial History*. Sharon Springs, NY: Sharon Historical Society, 1997.

Nichols, Preston. *The Montauk Project: Experiments in Time*. Westbury, NY: The Sky Press, 1992.

Noyes, George Wallingford. *Free Love in Utopia: John Humphrey Noyes and the Origin of the Oneida Community.* Urbana: University of Illinois Press, 2001.

Palmer, Richard. "Rise and Fall of Richburg." *Crooked Lake Review,* Spring-Summer, 2007.

Redfern, Nick. *Keep Out! Top Secret Places Governments Don't Want You to Know About.* Pompton Plains, NJ: The Career Press, 2012.

Reed, Jennifer Bond. *Love Canal.* Philadelphia: Chelsea House Publishers, 2002.

Seaver, James. *The Life of Mary Jemison: The White Woman of the Genesee.* 1824. Reprint, Scituate, MA: Digital Scanning, 2001.

Sherrow, Victoria. *Love Canal: Toxic Waste Tragedy.* Berkeley Heights, NJ: Enslow Publishers, 2001.

Stalter, Elizabeth "Perk." *Doodletown: Hiking Through History in a Vanished Hamlet on the Hudson.* Bear Mountain, NY: Palisades Interstate Park Commission Press, 1996.

Starbuck, David. *Massacre at Fort William Henry.* Lebanon, NH: University Press of New England, 2002.

——. *Rangers and Redcoats on the Hudson.* Lebanon, NH: University Press of New England, 2004.

Steele, Ian. *Betrayals: Fort William Henry and the "Massacre."* New York: University Press, 1990.

Steinberg, Davd. *Hiking the Road to Ruins: Day Trips and Camping Adventures to Iron Mines, Old Military Sites, and Things Abandoned in the New York City Area. . . and Beyond.* New Brunswick, NJ: Rivergate Books, 2007.

Stone, Darnall. "Acidalia and the Acid Factories." Unpublished article, undated.

Maritime Industry Museum at Fort Schuyler: Self-Guided Walking Tour. New York: Maritime Industry Museum at Fort Schuyler, 2005.

Various. *Former Settlements in New York.* Memphis, TN: General Books, 2010.

Wergland, Glendyne. *One Shaker Life: Isaac Newton Youngs, 1793-1865.* Boston: University of Massachusetts Press, 2006.

WEBSITES

The American Hotel. http://www.americanhotelny.com.

"Background Information." University at Buffalo Libraries Love Canal Collections. http://library.buffalo.edu/specialcollections/lovecanal/about/background.php.

"Battle for Fort Clinton." Son of the South. http://www.sonofthesouth.net/revolutionary-war/battles/battle-fort-clinton.htm.

"A Brief History of Roseton and Danskammer Point, NY." Brick Collecting. http://www.brickcollecting.com/roseton.htm.

Breslin, Tom. "St. Helena: 1797–1954." Glimpses of the Past: People, Places, and Things in Letchworth Park History. http://www.letchworthparkhistory.com/sthe.html.

"Brief History of Sharon Springs: Historic Mineral Spa Village." Sharon Springs Spas. http://sharonspringsspas.com/sharonsprings-history.htm.

"Brothers: NYC's Worst Maritime Tragedy." Forgotten New York. http://forgotten-ny.com/2004/09/north-brother-island/.

"Camp Santanoni Historic Area." New York State Department of Environmental Conservation. http://www.dec.ny.gov/lands/53095.html.

Cleveland Hill High School Advanced Placement History Class New Ireland, New York Project. http://home.comcast.net/~dickallen5/nycattar/new_ireland/NI_Index.html.

Cole, Sean. "How to Get to North Brother Island." Radiolab, November 15, 2011. http://www.radiolab.org/blogs/radiolab-blogland/2011/nov/15/how-get-north-brother-island/.

"Crown Point State Historic Site." Lake Champlain Region. http://www.lakechamplainregion.com/recreation/heritage/crown-point-state-historic-site.

"Fort Schuyler." New York State Military Museum and Veterans Research Center. http://www.dmna.ny.gov/forts/fortsQ_S/schuylerFort.htm.

"Fort Ticonderoga: America's Fort." Fort Ticonderoga. http://www.fortticonderoga.org.

Furness, Gregory T. "Crown Point." America's Historic Lakes: The Lake Champlain and Lake George Historic Site. http://www.historiclakes .org/crown_pt/furness.html.

Ghost Towns.com. http://www.ghosttowns.com.

Hamill, John. "Forts Clinton and Montgomery." John's Military History Page. http://www.johnsmilitaryhistory.com/Forts%20Clinton%20and %20Montgomery.html.

Hick, Charles S. "Rifle that Killed Sheriff Steele; O'Mearas First Irish Family." Town of Fremont. http://www.fremontnewyork.us/historypage 15.html.

"History and Culture." National Park Service: Ellis Island. http://www.nps .gov/elis/historyculture/index.htm.

"History of Fort Schuyler." Maritime College, State University of New York. http://www.sunymaritime.edu/Maritime%20Museum/Fort Schuyler/Index.aspx.

"A History of the McIntyre Mine." Adirondack History. http://www .adirondack-park.net/history/mcintyre.mine.html.

Horrigan, Jeremiah. "Land Purchase Trapps a Piece of History." *Times-Herald Record* (Middletown, New York), August 8, 2002. Last updated December 15, 2010. http://www.recordonline.com/apps/pbcs .dll/article?AID=/20020808/NEWS/308089990&cid=sitesearch.

Hunter, Dean. "Cannonsville, New York 1786–1956." Delaware County, NY Genealogy and History Site. http://www.dcnyhistory.org/ cannonsville17861956hunter.html.

Jackson, Nicholas. "On That Spooky New York Leper Colony Everyone is Talking About." *The Atlantic*, February 1, 2012. http://www.the atlantic.com/health/archive/2012/02/on-that-spooky-new-york-leper-colony-everyone-is-talking-about/252401/.

"Kings Park Psychiatric Center." Hours of Darkness: Modern Ruins Photography. http://www.hoursofdarkness.com/KPPC.htm.

"Kings Park Psychiatric Center—A Documentation." http://s.albalux.com/ webpage/main.html.

Kirsch, Tom. Riverside Hospital (North Brother Island). Opacity. http://www.opacity.us/site100_riverside_hospital_north_brother_island .htm.

"Letchworth Village." Asylum Projects. http://www.asylumprojects.org/ index.php?title=Letchworth_Village.

Levine, David. "Remembering Camp Shanks." *Hudson Valley Magazine*, August 16, 2010. http://www.hvmag.com/Hudson-Valley-Magazine/ September-2010/Remembering-Camp-Shanks/.

"Love Canal." Encyclopedia Britannica. http://www.britannica.com/ EBchecked/topic/349473/Love-Canal.

Metzger, Thom. "Transform and Rebel: The Calico Indians and the Anti-rent War." The Anarchist Library. http://theanarchistlibrary.org/library/thom-metzger-transform-and-rebel-the-calico-indians-and-the-anti-rent-war.

Miles, Hester Lane. "History of Cannonsville." Delaware County, NY Genealogy and History Site. http://www.dcnyhistory.org/cannon.html.

Mohonk Preserve. http://www.mohonkpreserve.org/.

"Mount Lebanon Shaker Society." National Park Service: Shaker Historic Trail. http://www.cr.nps.gov/nr/ travel/shaker/mou.htm.

"Mount Lebanon Shaker Village." World Monuments Fund. http://www.wmf.org/project/mount-lebanon-shaker-village.

"North Brother Island." Atlas Obscura. http://atlasobscura.com/place/north-brother-island.

"North Brother Island." Northbrotherislan.blogspot.com, April 26, 2007. http://northbrotherislan.blogspot.com/.

O'Donnell, Dr. Edward T. "General Slocum Disaster Remembered: 1904–2004." Juniper Park Civic Association. http://www.junipercivic.com/historyArticle.asp?nid=15.

"Oneida Community Mansion House: Still Perfect." Oneida Community Mansion House. http://www.oneidacommunity.org.

"Our History." Sharon Springs Chamber of Commerce. http://www.sharonspringschamber.com/ourhistory.html.

Reynoldston New York.org. http://www.reynoldstonnewyork.org/.

Riis, Jacob A. "Riverside Hospital New York City North Brother Island." *Cosmopolitan Magazine*, July 1902. Available at Digital History Project. http://www.digitalhistoryproject.com/2012/05/riverside-hospital-new-york-city-north.html.

Severo, Richard. "Revolutionary Fort Held Hostage to Decay and Apathy." *New York Times*, May 24, 1998. http://www.nytimes.com/1998/05/24/nyregion/revolutionary-fort-held-hostage-to-decay-and-apathy.html.

Shaker Museum/Mount Lebanon. http://www.shakermuseumandlibrary.org.

Smith, H. P. "Chapter III: Indian Relations in Central New York." In *History of Cortland County*, 26–34. Syracuse, NY: D. Mason & Co., 1885. Available at Rootsweb. http://www.usgenweb.info/nycortland/books/1885-3.htm.

———. "History of North Elba, NY." In *History of Essex County*. Syracuse, NY: D. Mason & Co., 1885. Available at Ray's Place. http://history.rays-place.com/ny/n-elba.htm.

"The Township of Red House." Rootsweb. http://www.rootsweb.ancestry.com/~nycattar/towns/redhouse.htm.

"West Point, New York." A Revolutionary Day along Historic US Route 9W. http://www.revolutionaryday.com/usroute9w/westpoint/default .htm.

Woolsey, Rebecca. "Feeble Science: Letchworth Village and Eugenics." Voices Like Yours, Spring 2007. http://voiceslikeyours.com/pdfs/ RWoolsey_FeebleScience.pdf.

INDEX